$33.70

Watergate

Other books in the At Issue in History series:

Watergate

William S. McConnell, *Book Editor*

Bruce Glassman, *Vice President*
Bonnie Szumski, *Publisher*
Helen Cothran, *Managing Editor*
Scott Barbour, *Series Editor*

 OPPOSING
VIEWPOINTS® AT ISSUE IN HISTORY
SERIES

GREENHAVEN PRESS
An imprint of Thomson Gale, a part of The Thomson Corporation

THOMSON
—————✳—————™
GALE

Detroit • New York • San Francisco • San Diego • New Haven, Conn.
Waterville, Maine • London • Munich

For more information, contact
Greenhaven Press
27500 Drake Rd.
Farmington Hills, MI 48331-3535
Or you can visit our Internet site at http://www.gale.com

Cover credit: © MPI/Hulton Archive by Getty Images. A demonstration in favor of President Nixon's impeachment takes place in front of the White House. Library of Congress, 15

LIBRARY OF CONGRESS CATALOGING-IN-PUBLICATION DATA

Watergate / William S. McConnell, book editor.
   p. cm. — (At issue in history)
Includes bibliographical references and index.
ISBN 0-7377-2691-1 (lib. : alk. paper)
   1. Watergate affair, 1972–1974. 2. Nixon, Richard M. (Richard Milhous), 1913–1994. 3. Mass media—Political aspects—United States. 4. United States—Politics and government—1969–1974. I. McConnell, William S. II. Series.
E860.W345 2006
973.924'092—dc22
                                        2005047194

Contents

Chapter 2: The Role of the Media in the Watergate Crisis

Chapter 3: The Legacy of Watergate

Foreword

Historian Robert Weiss defines history simply as "a record and interpretation of past events." Both elements—record and interpretation—are necessary, Weiss argues.

Names, dates, places, and events are the essence of history. But historical writing is not a compendium of facts. It consists of facts placed in a sequence to tell a connected story. A work of history is not merely a story, however. It also must analyze what happened and *why*—that is, it must interpret the past for the reader.

For example, the events of December 7, 1941, that led President Franklin D. Roosevelt to call it "a date which will live in infamy" are fairly well known and straightforward. A force of Japanese planes and submarines launched a torpedo and bombing attack on American military targets in Pearl Harbor, Hawaii. The surprise assault sank five battleships, disabled or sank fourteen additional ships, and left almost twenty-four hundred American soldiers and sailors dead. On the following day, the United States formally entered World War II when Congress declared war on Japan.

These facts and consequences were almost immediately communicated to the American people who heard reports about Pearl Harbor and President Roosevelt's response on the radio. All realized that this was an important and pivotal event in American and world history. Yet the news from Pearl Harbor raised many unanswered questions. Why did Japan decide to launch such an offensive? Why were the attackers so successful in catching America by surprise? What did the attack reveal about the two nations, their people, and their leadership? What were its causes, and what were its effects? Political leaders, academic historians, and students look to learn the basic facts of historical events and to read the intepretations of these events by many different sources, both primary and secondary, in order to develop a more complete picture of the event in a historical context.

    In the case of Pearl Harbor, several important questions surrounding the event remain in dispute, most notably the role of President Roosevelt. Some historians have blamed his policies for deliberately provoking Japan to attack in order to propel America into World War II; a few have gone so far as to accuse him of knowing of the impending attack but not informing others. Other historians, examining the same event, have exonerated the president of such charges, arguing that the historical evidence does not support such a theory.

    The Greenhaven At Issue in History series recognizes that many important historical events have been interpreted differently and in some cases remain shrouded in controversy. Each volume features a collection of articles that focus on a topic that has sparked controversy among eyewitnesses, contemporary observers, and historians. An introductory essay sets the stage for each topic by presenting background and context. Several chapters then examine different facets of the subject at hand with readings chosen for their diversity of opinion. Each selection is preceded by a summary of the author's main points and conclusions. A bibliography is included for those students interested in pursuing further research. An annotated table of contents and thorough index help readers to quickly locate material of interest. Taken together, the contents of each of the volumes in the Greenhaven At Issue in History series will help students become more discriminating and thoughtful readers of history.

Introduction

The presidency of Richard M. Nixon (1969–1974) is known for a number of notable foreign policy achievements. Nixon was the first democratic leader to visit the People's Republic of China and open negotiations leading to trade between that Communist nation and the Western world. To decrease Cold War fears over a nuclear war with the Soviet Union, Nixon also worked to achieve détente, a period of improved relations between the United States and the Soviet Union that began in 1971. These foreign policy initiatives helped to divert public attention from the increasingly unpopular Vietnam War and several domestic problems, including racial conflict and economic inflation. But Nixon's achievements could not outweigh the political scandal known as Watergate, which would forever be linked to his administration and which ultimately led to Nixon's resignation, the only presidential resignation in U.S. history.

Watergate involved several layers of political misconduct and conspiracy related to Nixon's successful campaign for reelection in 1972. It began with misuse of campaign funds and dirty tricks against political opponents, continued in 1973 with federal evidence tampering and obstruction of justice, and finally broadened into a national debate over abuse of power, government secrecy, antagonism between government and the media, and public mistrust of elected officials. It all started, however, with a surprisingly crude and bungled series of petty crimes.

CRP and the Plumbers Unit

One source of illegal activities was Nixon's Republican campaign organization, the Committee to Reelect the President (CRP, or "CREEP" to its critics). In addition to legitimate campaign activities, in 1972 members of CRP played a number of "dirty tricks," unethical acts ranging from practical jokes intended to embarrass the opposition to overtly illegal activities such as political espionage. One political strategist and member of CRP, Donald Segretti, who had a

10

long record of political smear tactics and was convicted of three misdemeanor counts of political misconduct, later testified at congressional hearings that his actions included "false pizza and liquor orders to campaign workers and [the posting of] bogus campaign posters,"[1] according to the *Washington Post.*

Another source of illegal activities was Nixon's White House staff. Within this group was a small circle dubbed the "plumbers," formed to stop leaks of information within the White House and to gather information against Nixon's political enemies. Among its operatives were G. Gordon Liddy, a member of CRP's finance committee, and James W. McCord Jr., a former Central Intelligence Agency operative and the current security consultant for CRP. White House chief of staff H.R. Haldeman, domestic affairs adviser John Ehrlichman, Attorney General Richard Kleindienst, and White House counsel John Dean and Egil Krogh variously planned, knew of, or covered up the plumbers' activities.

In 1971 the plumbers unit orchestrated the break-in of the office of psychiatrist Daniel Ellsberg, who had leaked sensitive documents to the *New York Times* regarding the Nixon administration's Vietnam War policy. In spring of 1972, the group planned to break into the offices of the Democratic National Committee (DNC) at the Watergate, a sprawling hotel and office-tower complex about a mile from the White House in Washington, D.C., in search of documents or information that would boost Nixon's campaign.

None of this was public knowledge and, at the time, few of these men questioned the legality or ethics of their acts. As Krogh later stated, "You can be vulnerable to pressure, particularly in a job like that when the president of the United States is asking you to do things. . . . I would have done anything—in fact I *did* anything—he [Nixon] asked me to do."[2]

Burglary at the Watergate Hotel

On June 17, 1972, a security guard named Frank Wills working the graveyard shift at the Watergate found evidence of a break-in while making his evening rounds. Several office doorknob cylinders were covered with masking tape to hold the doors open. Wills contacted the city police department, whose officers discovered and arrested five burglars inside the DNC offices on suspicion of illegal wiretapping. One of the arrested men was James McCord. Former attorney general and current director of CRP John Mitchell immediately issued a statement that the burglars "were not operating either on our behalf or with our consent in the alleged bugging attempt."[3]

At the request of the DNC, the Federal Bureau of Investigation opened an investigation into the incident, which led to the criminal indictment of seven men, including McCord, Liddy, and E. Howard Hunt Jr., a former White House security consultant. The indictments of McCord and Liddy provided investigators with a connection to Nixon's reelection campaign, while the indictment of Hunt provided investigators with a connection to the White House.

A few newspapers, notably the *Washington Post*, refused to let the story die. The *Post* began to publish more and more alarming reports of a broadening network of illegal activity. *Post* reporters Bob Woodward and Carl Bernstein wrote on October 11, 1972, that "hundreds of thousands of dollars in Nixon campaign contributions had been set aside to pay for an extensive undercover campaign aimed at discrediting individual Democratic presidential candidates and disrupting their campaigns . . . [and that] federal investigators said what they uncovered being done by the Nixon forces is unprecedented in scope and intensity."[4] Nixon and the high-ranking members of his reelection committee all denied any involvement in these activities, and in November Nixon won reelection in one of the biggest landslides in U.S. history, defeating Democrat George McGovern with over 60 percent of the popular vote and carrying forty-nine of the fifty states' electoral votes. However, on February 7, 1973, with questions still remaining regarding the president's knowledge of the Watergate affair, the Senate voted to establish the Senate Watergate Committee, which was charged with investigating the extent of campaign abuses in the 1972 presidential election.

Implicating the President

On May 18, 1973, the Senate Judiciary Committee appointed Texas attorney Archibald Cox as the special prosecutor charged with heading the investigation. The scope of Cox's investigation would cover not only the Watergate break-in but also any alleged misconduct surrounding CRP during the 1972 presidential election. On May 19, the Senate Watergate Committee began conducting televised hearings, dramatic proceedings that would rivet public attention for months.

Among early witnesses were several of the original defendants in the Watergate break-in case. Then, on June 3, former presidential counsel John Dean testified under oath that he had discussed the break-in and an attempt to cover up CRP's involvement with President Nixon at least thirty-five times. According to news reports of this bombshell,

> One of the strongest charges against Mr. Nixon that Dean has made to investigators refers to a meeting Dean said he had with Mr. Nixon shortly before the sentencing of the seven Watergate defendants March 23. Dean said that Mr. Nixon asked him how much the defendants would have to be paid to insure their continued silence, in addition to $460,000 that had already been paid. Dean maintains that he told Mr. Nixon the additional cost would be about $1 million, and Dean also claims the President replied there would be no problem in paying that amount.[5]

On July 10, John Mitchell denied any prior approval of the Watergate break-in. Then came another bombshell: On July 18, former White House aide Alexander Butterfield testified that "President Nixon has been routinely taping all his conversations and meetings in the Oval Office and cabinet room of the White House, in his Executive Office Building office and on four of his personal telephones."[6] The White House confirmed that such a taping system existed and that it had been in operation since 1971. The existence of a secret taping system had serious implications for the investigation. If Nixon truly was innocent, then the proof would be somewhere in the taped conversations.

The Saturday Night Massacre

Once the existence of the secret White House taping system was revealed by the press, special prosecutor Archibald Cox subpoenaed the tapes from President Nixon. Nixon flatly refused the subpoena by stating,

> The tapes are entirely consistent with what I know to be the truth and what I have stated to be the truth. However, as in any verbatim recording of informal

conversations, they contain comments that persons with different perspectives and motivations would inevitably interpret in different ways. Furthermore, there are inseparably interspersed in them a great many very frank and very private comments on a wide range of issues and individuals, wholly extraneous to the Committee's inquiry.[7]

Nixon's refusal to deliver the tapes set the stage for a tense legal standoff between the Senate Watergate Committee, Cox, and the White House. The committee chair, North Carolina senator Sam Ervin, reacted to the president's decision by saying, "I deeply regret that this situation has arisen, because I think that the Watergate tragedy is the greatest tragedy this country has ever suffered. I used to think that the Civil War was our country's greatest tragedy, but I do remember that there were some redeeming features in the Civil War in that there was some spirit of sacrifice and heroism displayed on both sides. I see no redeeming features in Watergate."[8]

The committee hearings continued while the issue of subpoenaed tapes went to the Supreme Court. A frustrated Nixon continued to receive and deny requests for tapes from Cox. Then, on October 20, 1973, Nixon demanded that Cox make no further attempts to subpoena White House tapes. When Cox refused, Nixon demanded that Attorney General Elliot L. Richardson fire Cox. Richardson refused to comply with the directive and resigned from his post. Nixon then asked Deputy Attorney General William D. Ruckelshaus to fire Cox. He too refused and resigned rather than comply with the presidential order. Finally, Solicitor General Robert H. Bork, who became acting attorney general in the wake of the resignations, carried out Nixon's order to fire Cox. In a letter to Bork, the president wrote, "Cox made it apparent that he will not comply with the instructions I issued to him. . . . Clearly the government of the United States cannot function if employees of the executive branch are free to ignore in this fashion the instructions of the President."[9] With this dramatic event, quickly dubbed the Saturday Night Massacre, the Watergate scandal became a major crisis in government.

Nixon abolished the office of the special prosecutor and turned over the Watergate investigation to the Justice Department. The Justice Department wasted no time in appointing a new special prosecutor. By naming Texas attorney Leon Jaworski to replace Cox as special prosecutor, the department clearly distanced itself from charges that it was a pawn of the president, much to the displeasure of Nixon. Jaworski continued the Senate's investigation and the requests to subpoena the secret White House tapes, although his investigation was now within the oversight of the House Judiciary Committee.

Transcripts Versus Tapes

The end of 1973 was filled with controversy over the subpoenaed tapes. In testimony before U.S. District Court judge John J. Sirica, White House chief of staff Alexander Haig (who had recently replaced Haldeman in the post) stated that one of the tapes containing conversations regarding the Watergate break-in had accidentally been erased. The White House was reluctant to release this tape, as it contained an eighteen-and-a-half-minute gap that could be misconstrued as an act of sabotage by the Nixon administration. This revelation did indeed increase the public's distrust of Nixon. Haig stated that the erasure was caused when Nixon's secretary, Rosemary Woods,

Richard M. Nixon

accidentally pressed "record" while on a telephone call. However, Woods testified under oath that she may have caused a five-minute erasure at the most, since she caught her mistake when she finished the phone conversation, and could not have caused the entire gap in the tape. Most of the investigators and the public at large did not believe Haig's testimony explaining how the tape came to be erased.

On April 29, 1974, Nixon delivered a speech to the American people in which he stated that he would release eighteen hundred pages of transcripts in lieu of the subpoenaed tapes. He explained that the transcripts had been edited in order to protect conversations regarding national security. Nixon acknowledged that "my effort to protect the confidentiality of Presidential conversations has heightened the sense of mystery about Watergate and, in fact, has caused increased suspicions of the President. Many people assume that the tapes must incriminate the President, or that otherwise, he would not insist on their privacy."[10]

Nixon believed that these edited transcripts would vindicate him, but the exchange of one form of evidence for another simply implicated him further in the eyes of many Americans. House Speaker Carl Albert criticized the use of transcripts by asking, "Why substitute other evidence when the direct evidence [the actual tapes] is available?"[11] Also, according to *Washington Post* reporter Haynes Johnson, when the transcripts were examined, evidence was found to show "Nixon discussing at length raising blackmail money; discussing the merits of offering clemency or parole; suggesting how to handle possible perjury or obstruction of justice charges; urging the adoption of a 'national security' defense for potential White House defendants."[12] Unfortunately, the transcripts were edited to such a degree that any direct reference to Watergate was missing. This fact outraged the House Judiciary Committee, which continued to demand that the actual tapes be released. The transcripts were also made available to the public, who generally distrusted Nixon more.

The Smoking Gun

On July 24, 1974, the Supreme Court finally ruled in favor of the House Judiciary Committee's subpoena: Nixon was constitutionally obliged to turn over the tapes. Nixon's lawyer James D. St. Clair had argued that the tapes were confidential under the claim of executive privilege, the concept that private discussions between the president and his staff receive the same legal protection as discussions between an attorney and his or her client. Writing for the Court, however, Chief Justice Warren E. Burger stated that,

> [executive] privilege depends solely on the broad, undifferentiated claim of public interest in the confidentiality of such conversations. . . . Absent a claim of need to protect military, diplomatic or sensitive national security secrets, we find it difficult to accept the argument that even the very important interest in confidentiality of Presidential communications is significantly dimin-

ished. . . . Since we conclude that the legitimate needs of the judicial process may outweigh Presidential privilege, it is necessary to resolve those competing interests in a manner that preserves the essential functions of each branch.[13]

Indeed, the tapes revealed that Nixon knew of the attempts to cover up the Watergate break-in as early as March 21, 1973. The tapes revealed not only the discussion regarding the payment of hush money to the conspirators, but also Nixon's demand that his closest staff members resign and that his name never come up in connection with any knowledge of activities involving Watergate. With this new evidence in hand, even Nixon's staunchest supporters questioned the actions of the president and called for his impeachment. A few days later, the House Judiciary Committee drew up three articles of impeachment charging Nixon with abuse of power and obstruction of justice.

Nixon's Resignation and American Cynicism Toward Government

Faced with an impeachment trial in the Senate, Nixon delivered his last public address as president of the United States on the evening of August 8, 1974. In a calm voice he stated,

> From the discussions I have had with Congressional and other leaders, I have concluded that because of the Watergate matter I might not have the support of the Congress that I would consider necessary to back the very difficult decisions and carry out the duties of this office in the way the interests of the Nation would require. . . . Therefore, I shall resign the Presidency effective at noon tomorrow. Vice President [Gerald] Ford will be sworn in as President at that hour in this office. . . . By taking this action, I hope that I will have hastened the start of that process of healing which is so desperately needed in America.[14]

Healing was not soon in coming, however, especially when one month later President Ford pardoned Nixon for any and all crimes that he may have committed while serving as president.

Nixon's handling of Watergate had a tremendous impact on the public's perception of the presidency. According to historian Stanley I. Kutler, "Americans alternately inflicted anger and derision on the office and the man. Ford's pardon added an element of cynicism. . . . Once peerless and invincible, presidential majesty seemed diminished, and Nixon and his immediate successors served as easy prey for cruel, even contemptuous humor."[15] The American people were less confident in their government's ability to solve problems and in elected officials' ethical and professional standards. Moreover, Watergate ushered in an era of so-called attack journalism—the media aggressively sought to investigate and discredit public officials, and the line between private and public conduct blurred. The White House–press corps relationship in particular took on a permanently adversarial tone.

Informational Leaks and the Press

Secret sources of information often play an important role in a journalist's ability to break important news stories to the public. Journalists protect their sources of information by promising not to reveal their identities, even under oath or threat of incarceration. Nixon's involvement in Watergate might never have been known if not for the key information provided by one such anonymous source, dubbed "Deep Throat."

During 1972, few newspapers were interested in pursuing the Watergate story at first. There was little evidence pointing to a conspiracy. Then *Washington Post* reporters Bob Woodward and Carl Bernstein were contacted by a source who claimed to have inside knowledge of Nixon's involvement. According to their book *All the President's Men*,

> Woodward had a source in the Executive Branch who had access to information at CREEP as well as at the White House. His identity was unknown to anyone else. He could be contacted only on very important occasions. Woodward had promised he would never identify him or his position to anyone. Further, he had agreed never to quote the man, even as an anonymous source. Their discussions would be only to confirm information that had been obtained elsewhere and to add some perspective.[16]

With the help of Deep Throat, the two *Post* reporters were

able to piece together the parts of the Watergate story, including Nixon's involvement.

For thirty years, this important source's name was never revealed. In an interview in 2005 with television news correspondent Tom Brokaw, Woodward revealed the elaborate schemes that he and Deep Throat employed to arrange a meeting. "If Deep Throat wanted to meet, he would draw a clock on page 20 of The New York Times delivered each day to [my] apartment. Deep Throat began insisting on meeting at 2 A.M. in a parking garage in Rosslyn, Virginia, just across the Potomac River from Washington. He ordered me to change cabs on my way there, to walk the last several blocks, and to make sure I wasn't being tailed."[17] In these secret meetings, Deep Throat confirmed such important information as CRP's involvement in a dirty tricks campaign, the involvement of key Nixon staff members, Haldeman's role as an organizer of the Watergate break-in, and the existence of secret taped conversations. He even cautioned Woodward that wiretapping had been ordered against the reporters. Without the secret meetings, Woodward and Bernstein might never have gained the confirmation of other facts needed to tie Nixon to Watergate.

Deep Throat Revealed

Bob Woodward remained true to his promise never to reveal the name of his most important source, but in May 2005 that source came forward on his own. In a *Vanity Fair* interview, former deputy director of the FBI Mark Felt, now ninety-one, revealed that he was Deep Throat. Woodward verified Felt's claim shortly after the *Vanity Fair* article was published. Felt's revelation was not entirely a surprise. In the secretly taped conversations in Nixon's office, Nixon and Dean discussed damaging leaks and named Felt as a possible source. Also, in 1976, according to reporter Nob Thompson, assistant attorney general Stanley Pottinger asked Felt under oath, "'Were you Deep Throat?' Felt initially said, 'No,' but his stunned look alerted Pottinger to the probability that he was lying. . . . Pottinger quietly reminded Felt that he was under oath. He then offered to withdraw the question as irrelevant to the subject of investigation, which was illegal break-ins conducted by the FBI . . . Felt quickly accepted the offer."[18]

A recent court decision makes it more difficult to protect sources' anonymity. On June 28, 2005, the Supreme Court ruled that journalists are not protected under the law and may be penalized if they refuse to reveal their sources. According to the Associated Press, this decision will have a stifling effect with terrible consequences for the public's ability to assess governmental actions: "Important information will be lost to the public if journalists cannot reliably promise anonymity to sources."[19] Had such a ruling been handed down at the time of the Watergate investigation, it is interesting to consider whether Felt would have played his role in Watergate, and if not, how the course of U.S. history might have differed.

Post-Watergate Changes

Besides its effect on public perception of government, Watergate had important, lasting effects on governmental processes. Campaign finance laws were reformed to prevent incumbents from outspending new political candidates who lacked the financial capital to compete with their more established opponents. The Freedom of Information Act gave ordinary citizens unprecedented access to government records and declassified huge amounts of information, in an effort to increase transparency in government. Watergate even changed the language of political scandal. Reflecting its significance, many scandals that followed garnered the *-gate* suffix: Irangate, Whitewatergate, Oilgate, and Filegate. Watergate thus not only brought down a presidency but changed the American political process.

Notes

1. *Washington Post*, "Segretti Testifies About 'Dirty Tricks,'" October 11, 1973.
2. Quoted in Kathy George, "Nixon Plumber Who Went to Prison Tells Story," *Seattle Post-Intelligencer*, September 15, 2003.
3. Quoted in Bob Woodward and Carl Bernstein, "GOP Security Aide Among Five Arrested in Bugging Affair," *Washington Post*, June 19, 1972.
4. Bob Woodward and Carl Bernstein, "FBI Nixon Aides Sabotaged Democrats," *Washington Post*, October 10, 1972.
5. Carl Bernstein and Bob Woodward, "Dean Alleges

Nixon Knew of Cover-Up Plan," *Washington Post*, June 3, 1973.

6. Quoted in Lawrence Meyer, "President Taped Talks, Phone Calls; Lawyer Ties Ehrlichman to Payments; Principal Offices Secretly Bugged Since Spring 1971," *Washington Post*, July 17, 1973.

7. Richard M. Nixon, "Letter to the Senate Watergate Committee," July 23, 1973.

8. Quoted in Carroll Kilpatrick, "President Refuses to Turn Over Tapes; Ervin Committee, Cox Issue Subpoenas; Action Sets Stage for Court Battle on Powers Issue," *Washington Post*, July 24, 1973.

9. Richard M. Nixon, "Letter to Solicitor General Robert H. Bork," October 20, 1973.

10. Richard M. Nixon, "Radio and Television Address to the American Public," April 29, 1974.

11. Quoted in Haynes Johnson, "President Hands Over Transcripts; Initial Reaction on Hill Divided Along Party Lines," *Washington Post*, May 1, 1974.

12. Johnson, "President Hands Over Transcripts."

13. Warren E. Berger, *United States v. Nixon* (1974), www.landmarkcases.org.

14. Richard M. Nixon, "Resignation Speech," August 8, 1974.

15. Stanley I. Kutler, *The Wars of Watergate: The Last Crisis of Richard Nixon.* New York: Alfred A. Knopf, 1990.

16. Carl Bernstein and Bob Woodward, *All the President's Men.* New York: Simon & Schuster, 1974.

17. Tom Brokaw, "The Secret Man, an Interview with Bob Woodward," *CBS News*, July 6, 2005.

18. Nob Thompson, "Deep Throat Source of Countless Guesses," *Washington Post*, July 1, 2005.

19. Associated Press, "Supreme Court Won't Protect Sources in CIA Leak," June 6, 2005. www.newsmax.com.

Chapter 1

A Presidency on Trial

1

A National Crisis Justifies Illegal Means to Win Reelection

Keith W. Olson

One of the most distressing aspects of the Watergate scandal was the public's perception that the president had broken laws not in the national interest but to maintain and protect his political power. The Nixon administration cast the situation differently. Richard Nixon and his advisers and campaign staff justified spying on Democratic candidates, amassing slush funds, and employing political dirty tricks as minor transgressions intended to prevent a liberal Democratic administration from derailing Nixon's Vietnam and economic policy programs. Thus, the break-in to the offices of the Democratic National Committee at the Watergate complex was approved, and then covered up, in the interest of national security. In the following excerpt from his book *Watergate: The Presidential Scandal That Shook America*, University of Maryland professor Keith W. Olson examines how extreme loyalty to Nixon influenced his staff members to break laws and cover up his actions. Olson argues, however, that Nixon's rationale was simply unconvincing, and that the public viewed Watergate as one in a series of criminal activities that brought down the Nixon presidency.

<hr>

W hen [Richard M.] Nixon became president he understood well the foreign policy of his four predecessors and their core belief that anticommunism sanctified exag-

Keith W. Olson, *Watergate: The Presidential Scandal That Shook America*. Lawrence: University Press of Kansas, 2003. Copyright © 2003 by the University Press of Kansas. All rights reserved. Reproduced by permission.

gerations, rigged elections, and cover-ups. An astute politician, Nixon had observed American presidents since 1946, and, indeed, for eight years as vice president stood ready to replace one should the need arise. He knew how the system worked.

President Nixon and his aides believed the nation faced a crisis at home that imperiled national and world security. Intercontinental ballistic missiles had eradicated the distinction between national and world safety, and these men believed Nixon's leadership was critical. Despite lack of evidence to support his position, the president remained convinced that communists were behind the anti-Vietnam protests. While talking to [Nixon's assistant for domestic affairs] John Ehrlichman on September 8, 1972, Nixon called his Democratic presidential opponent, George McGovern, a "Communist sonofabitch." Within the White House, the objective of ensuring Nixon's reelection justified strong measures, because, as his adviser and speechwriter Patrick Buchanan told him in March 1971, if he lost, "we all go, and maybe the country with us." With Nixon's approval, Buchanan and others set about to prevent that loss. A year later Buchanan reported to Attorney General John Mitchell and Nixon's chief of staff, H.R. Haldeman, that "our primary objective to prevent Senator Muskie from sweeping the early primaries . . . and uniting the Democratic party behind him for the fall, has been achieved." Buchanan recommended as their next step that they assist George McGovern in his bid for the Democratic nomination "in every way we can." Looking back, William Safire, one of three Nixon speechwriters, admitted the obvious when he wrote, "Watergate was essentially an abuse of the power of the government in order to affect an election." Charles Colson later explained Watergate as the result of White House officials believing illegal actions were "necessary for the president to survive and [they] covered their own misdeeds while rationalizing it all as being in the interests of the country."

The Threat of Communism
Justified Illegal Activities

Nixon's two closest political associates left vivid accounts of their reasoning that the end justified illegal means in winning the election of 1972. In February of that year Haldeman declared on national television that the critics of

Nixon's Vietnam policy "now are consciously aiding and abetting the enemy of the United States." These critics included former vice president Hubert Humphrey and Senators Edmund Muskie, Ted Kennedy, and George McGovern. Haldeman believed that "the President's critics are in favor of putting a Communist government in South Vietnam." Haldeman's belief that the leading Democratic candidates for their party's presidential nomination were traitors thus validated his illegal activities during the 1972 campaign and his later obstruction of justice and perjury.

Haldeman's belief that the leading Democratic candidates for their party's presidential nominations were traitors thus validated his illegal activities during the 1972 campaign.

On July 10, 1973, when John Mitchell testified before the Senate Watergate Committee, he explained why he withheld information about the Watergate break-in from the police and the FBI; why he failed to report information about Donald Segretti's dirty tricks campaign that Mitchell called "the White House Horrors"; and why he did not report information about individuals who he knew had committed perjury to cover up these crimes. One committee member reminded Mitchell that during the 1972 campaign he knew that Magruder, Haldeman, Ehrlichman, and persons "all around" the president were "involved in crime, perjury, accessory after the fact, and you deliberately refused to tell" Nixon. The senator then asked the former attorney general, "Would you state that the expediency of the election was more important than that?" Mitchell replied, "Senator, I think you have put it exactly correct. In my mind, the reelection of Richard Nixon, compared with what was available on the other side, was so much more important that I put it in just that context." The next day Mitchell testified again and repeated the logic behind his perjury and obstruction of justice: "The most important thing to this country was the reelection of Richard Nixon and I was not about to countenance anything that would stand in the way of that reelection." Mitchell apparently missed the irony that CREEP [the Committee to Re-Elect the President] and

Nixon's aides maneuvered covertly to have the Democratic Party nominate McGovern.

Mitchell's testimony articulated the dominant philosophy of the Nixon reelection campaign. Second only to the president with responsibility to enforce the law, Mitchell preferred, and helped plan, an unfair election rather than accept the prospect of voters electing a Democratic president in an honest election. Nor were Nixon's aides alone in their philosophy. Top executives in eighteen of the nation's best-known corporations made illegal campaign contributions to give Nixon a secret, unfair advantage. Once a corporate leader or a presidential aide accepted the basic premise that a Nixon defeat would damage the national interest, the other activities justifiably followed. The atmosphere that Cold War presidents created while conducting foreign policy and, more important, internal secret policy made Watergate possible.

Watergate Break-In Viewed as an Acceptable Campaign Tactic

In addition to national interest in the broader world perspective, the loose ethics of American political campaigns helps to explain the manifestations of Watergate. The Nixon White House often blurred the line between criminality and accepted campaign tactics. The tape of June 23, 1972, that Nixon fought so hard to keep, the tape that indeed was the smoking gun that his defenders insisted investigators must produce, recorded a conversation between Haldeman and the president. On the tape Nixon and his chief of staff discussed having the CIA director Richard Helms tell the FBI director L. Patrick Gray to stay away from investigating the Watergate break-in. Then, Nixon said, "All right, fine. How do you call him in—I mean you just—well, we protected Helms from one hell of a lot of things." One implication is obvious. Helms and the CIA had carried out activities that exceeded his and the agency's authority, and Nixon had covered them up.

For Nixon, a cover-up of unauthorized operations was nothing new when he and his aides embarked on the Watergate cover-up. Indeed, Jeb Stuart Magruder later remembered the cover-up as "immediate and automatic; no one ever considered that there would not be a cover-up." Haldeman did not view a political burglary as anything exceptional. To Nixon's speechwriter Ray Price, Haldeman later recalled "the unimportance of it in our minds at the time it happened" and added that Watergate was "really only one of maybe fifteen things we were honing in on that day." A burglary, even in the headquarters of the opposition party, and its subsequent cover-up seemed so commonplace to Nixon and his various appointees that they completely underestimated its potential for disaster.

Americans believed that if Nixon really wanted to end the Watergate controversy, as he insisted he did, he would have released the tapes. . . . Common sense defeated Nixon.

Americans have tolerated campaign activities that sometimes transgress accepted norms of decency and violate the spirit and, at times, the letter of the law. Three examples illustrate this point: Lyndon Johnson won his first Senate seat with voter tabulations manipulated to provide him with a winning margin; until the 1965 Voting Rights Act, local jurisdictions and states across the South routinely denied their black citizens the right to vote; and in 1952 the Republican Party platform maintained that "successive Democratic Administrations . . . have shielded traitors to the Nation in high places." The burglary did not shock Americans, which was one reason George McGovern could never turn it into an important issue during the 1972 campaign. Although the break-in, combined with the earlier dirty tricks, strained the outer limits of acceptability, they would not have driven Nixon from office when disclosed, unless he personally had orchestrated most of them. The public, moreover, would have accepted a cover-up, and even misinformation or lies, if a president could demonstrate that such actions had served the national interest. Nixon and his aides believed his reelection was indispensable to the national interest and hence justified the use of the CIA to block the investigation of the Watergate burglary and all other aspects of the cover-up. Americans interpreted the matter differently; they saw it as an attempt to promote and protect Nixon's political career.

At several instances between June 1972 and July 1973, Nixon could have taken decisive actions to defuse Watergate. After the break-in he could have declared his own innocence and fired Mitchell, Magruder, Haldeman, and Ehrlichman. No one ever contemplated such a measure because the break-in fell within accepted political campaign behavior. . . .

Throughout the entire Watergate affair, Nixon believed he had acted within the American presidential political system because he used his power to protect and promote the national interest; he acknowledged only "mistakes and misjudgments." Nixon and his assistants interpreted the anti-Vietnam campaign and the 1960s' cultural revolution as threats to national stability and to U.S. leadership in the world. To counter these perceived national threats, he instinctively reacted according to prevailing political presidential values. In this respect, Watergate constituted a chapter in the history of what [historian and social critic] Arthur M. Schlesinger Jr. has called "the imperial presidency." The reaction of the nation to President Johnson's imperial presidency should have served as a warning to Nixon, but it did not.

Nixon's Two Mistakes

Nixon made two glaring mistakes. First, he operated on the belief that foreign and domestic affairs and policies were inseparable and could be dealt with in the same manner. His predecessors repeatedly expressed such beliefs, and historians consistently emphasize the relationship between domestic conditions and foreign affairs. When Nixon related the domestic mood and activities to the nation's image and role in the world, therefore, he acted within the intellectual framework of post–World War II history. His mistake was the unsubtle application of that belief in specific instances, such as the burglary of the office of Daniel Ellsburg's psychiatrist,[1] the suborning of testimony to protect the cover-up, and the attempt to have the CIA block the FBI investigation of the Watergate break-in. In these instances the vast majority of Americans, it turned out, did not see the connection between domestic and foreign affairs.

Nixon's second glaring mistake was his systematic lying

---

1. H.R. Haldeman and Charles Colson initiated a break-in into this office to search for incriminating evidence for the Daniel Ellsburg trial. Daniel Ellsburg released top-secret documents to the *Washington Post* regarding U.S. policy in Vietnam. They became known as the Pentagon Papers.

between the beginning of the cover-up and the resignation. This lying, when exposed, combined with his persistent refusal to release the tapes that most Americans believed would reveal the truth about Watergate, led to Nixon's resignation. The country's earlier post–World War II presidents had lied to the public, but none ever did so in such detail, so often, and over such a long period of time. Nixon strained the nation's patience; the cover-up lasted too long. Americans believed that if Nixon really wanted to end the Watergate controversy, as he insisted he did, he would have released the tapes. His citing of abstract principles sounded unconvincing. Common sense defeated Nixon. . . .

Up to a point, Nixon's actions were not aberrations. The Watergate break-in and the dirty tricks campaign fit within the context of internal security policies with which Nixon and his aides were familiar. By itself, exposure of the dirty tricks would not have led to Nixon's, or any other president's, resignation. Executives at American Airlines, Goodyear Rubber, and sixteen other corporations secretly and illegally contributed funds to give Nixon an unfair advantage in the 1972 campaign. They, like the president and his aides, assumed that the ends justified the means. In 1964 and 1968 President Johnson tapped the office and plane telephones of the Republican presidential candidates. In 1972 the Committee to Re-elect the President did the tapping instead of the FBI. Nixon expected the director of the CIA to cover up for him in return for past protection. With the CIA's budget both generous and removed from congressional debate, the protection Nixon gave apparently related to Helms's acting beyond his constitutional authority.

Watergate Reflected Cold War Policies

Above all, Watergate was a predictable, though unique, expression of the contours of American politics, the imperial presidency, during the Cold War. The president, constitutionally empowered to conduct foreign affairs and to command the armed forces, came to dominate politics during a bipolar era when either of two nations could destroy much of the world. Each president through that time believed covert activity necessary, and each relied on oversimplification, exaggeration, and crisis analysis as an operational philosophy. Throughout this period the influence of the National Security Council, the CIA, the FBI, and the White

House staff steadily increased. So did surveillance. . . .

In planning the 1972 campaign, Nixon's aides adopted measures "to affect an election," as William Safire later wrote. Nixon's top campaign managers approved disruption of primary campaigns and elections, dissemination of false information, and intelligence gathering. To block investigation of the failed June 1972 burglary, Haldeman immediately thought of assistance from the CIA. Nixon's aides instinctively covered up their illegal campaign activities. Ultimately, they explained that the reelection of the president was in the national interest, and that justified whatever steps they deemed necessary.

The patterns of their thinking and their activities mirrored those of U.S. officials during the Cold War. In an atmosphere of oversimplification, exaggeration, and crisis analysis, a noble end justified illegal means. To an extent, Watergate was an expression of foreign policy at home. None of this excuses or defends Nixon's actions or those of his aides. Domestic conditions and foreign policy, indeed, are interrelated, but Watergate clearly demonstrated that Americans will accept executive actions in other countries that they will not accept at home. Nixon and his aides went beyond the pale of public acceptance with the illegal Plumbers [code name in the White House Special Investigation Unit] and their burglaries, the obstruction of justice, the subornation of testimony and commitment of perjury, and the abuse of federal agencies. For their inadequate sense of limits and their lack of respect for due process at home, Nixon and his aides paid a price. Nixon lost his presidency and accepted a pardon from his successor; eighteen of his aides went to prison. An analysis of Nixon's role in Watergate framed in the context of the Cold War demands a broader and deeper indictment than merely that of his being the first president to resign from office.

2
Nixon Should Resign
to Silence His Critics

William F. Buckley Jr.

Between October 1972 and May 1973, the White House co-operated to a limited extent with the House Judiciary Committee, the congressional committee charged with collecting evidence to determine if President Nixon had knowledge of the break-in of the Democratic National Committee offices at the Watergate office complex. Even the limited documents handed over to the committee were damning: Based on a letter from Nixon aide James W. McCord to Judge John J. Sirica stating that McCord had lied in court when he denied Nixon's knowledge of the cover-up, on statements from Nixon special counsel John Dean that implicated the White House, and on Nixon's own refusal to cooperate with the House Judiciary Committee, it was becoming more evident that Nixon did indeed have knowledge of the incident and may have even condoned its cover-up as an attempt to protect his presidency.

In the following *National Review* editorial from November 9, 1973, the magazine's founding publisher, conservative commentator William F. Buckley Jr., argues that Nixon has lost some of his legitimacy as a leader. Buckley implies that the evidence against Nixon has been exaggerated by members of the liberal press, but suggests that the president's resignation may be the only way to restore public confidence in the office of the president. William F. Buckley Jr. is the author of more than forty books and was the host for more than thirty years of the political talk show *Firing Line*. His newspaper column "On the Right" is syndicated in more than three hundred newspapers.

*N*R [*National Review*] has always thought the fuss over the [secret White House] tapes, on both sides, much exaggerated. It has seemed to us probable that, even if unaltered, the tapes would turn out to be, as the President stated, ambiguous and "capable of differing interpretations," as are most things human beings say to each other. It was a quirk of history that the tapes got blown up like Desdemona's handkerchief.

Richard Nixon is still the legal head of government, but is he, in the meaning proper to a constitutional, republican society, still a legitimate *ruler?*

Many, even most, of the individual items are trivial, but, in spite of Zeno's paradox, a great many trivialities can add up to something important. And it is not a matter of quantity alone. The central question raised by the past six months is that of the nature, the over-all quality, of the Nixon regime, and the further question, dependent on the first, of Nixon's ability to govern the country—govern it not in the purely formal sense, which, since we are not at the edge of revolution, our stable institutions assure, but in a manner consonant with the security and voluntary consent and well-being and peace of mind of the citizenry. In short: Richard Nixon is still the legal head of government, but is he, in the meaning proper to a constitutional, republican society, still a *legitimate* ruler?

Nixon Had Some Knowledge of Illegal Activities

The day-by-day Watergate developments have been so multitudinous and so rapidly changing as to benumb the mind and obscure the larger pattern. If we stop to look above the details, the present situation of the Nixon government is really preposterous. Every single one of the President's intimate aides and advisers (except [Secretary of State Henry] Kissinger, who is in an unrelated category) has been thrown to the wolves, along with key Cabinet members and the Vice President he had twice chosen, and most lately still another Attorney General and the special prosecutor he had appointed supposedly to clean up the mess. Harassed by the relentless guerrilla thrusts of the media, the President has for months been fighting his own legalistic and political guerrilla war from semi-hiding against the legislature, the courts, and even much of the executive branch to hamper or block disclosure of what his colleagues, aides, and he himself have been up to. In spite of the media's provocations, "preposterous" is an appropriate word by which to describe the President's screening operation, since it is he who, by normal rules, should have been heading the search rather than trying to divert, confuse, and suppress it.

The President's strategy has been based on the expectation that, as nearly every issue does in our volatile society, it would soon blow over, that the public would become bored and would stop wallowing in Watergate.

Many citizens believe: a) that the President knew about many of the improper and illegal actions, including many still unrevealed, even if he did not specifically initiate them; b) that he in any case bears a general responsibility for the activities of so numerous a band of his entourage; c) that he has perverted, or tried to pervert, agencies of government, including the IRS, the Justice Department, and, most important, the FBI and CIA—that is, the domestic and foreign security agencies—to serve partisan and personal aims; d) that he has tried to cover up the improper and illegal acts of his associates and is himself guilty of improper, degrading, and quite probably illegal acts; e) that he has tried to put himself above and beyond the law; f) that he has lost his credibility.

The accumulated unease with Mr. Nixon's person and conduct was triggered into a massive and somewhat hysterical explosion by the firing of Special Prosecutor Archibald Cox and the decapitation of the Justice Department. For the first time the question of impeachment began to be widely and seriously posed, and the rising tumult was checked, somewhat, only by the President's abrupt turn and apparent surrender to Judge Sirica on one sector of the "privilege" front.

If Mr. Nixon is in direct defiance of the courts—as for

three days he undoubtedly was—and persists in that defiance; or if one or another of the investigations and judicial inquiries comes up with firm evidence of his guilt in one or more crimes, then Congress will most certainly have to impeach him, in spite of all the awkwardness of the impeachment process. But the problem is not just one of direct defiance or presumptive legal guilt. This country is in the midst of a classic *crise de régime*, and the basic issue, as we have said, is the credibility and legitimacy of the head of government. From the beginning of the Watergate affair, the President's strategy has been based on the expectation that, as nearly every issue does in our volatile society, it would soon blow over, that the public would become bored and would stop wallowing in Watergate. But it has not blown over, and he, as well as the public, is wallowing. The downward plunge of confidence in the President from its post-election high has not noticeably reversed in response to any of his moves. Perhaps the surrender on the tapes will prove a turning point, but if not (as is more likely) and if the public distrust and rejection of Mr. Nixon persists, depends further, and hardens, the country will be facing the crippling and possibly catastrophic prospect of three years without— a legitimate government.

Resignation Is a Suitable Alternative

The one way and the only way to close out that crisis would be by Richard Nixon's departure. Though the Constitution prescribes, only the single, very nearly useless, and in this case presumably catatonic process of impeachment for bringing that departure about, there is another much simpler and far less traumatic method entirely consistent with the Constitution: Richard Nixon's resignation. If Mr. Nixon becomes convinced—and by a few more months at most it will be sure, one way or another—that he has irretrievably lost the support and trust of a solid majority of the people, it will then be his duty to resign his office as the only act able to heal the grievous wound. This would be, under the circumstances, the highest act of loyalty and patriotism on his part, and we therefore feel that Richard Nixon, facing the reality, would see resignation as his duty; and if he did not, it would become the duty of his closest friends and associates to persuade him so to see it.

In presenting the possibility of resignation, we assume,

of course, the presence of a Vice President who would succeed. More than 60 per cent of the electorate declared its support of the general line of policy they believe to be Mr. Nixon's, and there is no reason to suppose they have changed their minds in that respect, no matter what may have happened to their judgments of Mr. Nixon himself. A Nixon resignation would therefore presuppose congressional confirmation of a Vice President. From a policy standpoint, Gerald Ford sufficiently meets the terms. If Mr. Nixon actually did decide on resignation before Ford's confirmation, and there was serious objection to Ford's becoming President, Mr. Nixon could surely come to a prior agreement with Congress—and with Gerald Ford—on an alternative, if there is felt to be one more able to reunite the government and the nation. The citizens, we feel sure, would not tolerate cheap partisan politics by Congress in such an event.

But if, by the New Year say, no charge of criminal conduct against the President takes unequivocal and public form, and at the same time he makes real progress in regaining the confidence of his countrymen, it will then be time for his critics, and especially his critics in Congress, to put up or shut up. Congress, then, should either stop talking about impeachment and in general stop the wallowing, or vote the impeachment and render the judgment. And if, then, Congress refused either to act or to subside, the President should force the issue and compel Congress to act on impeachment once and for all.

3

Tape Transcripts Prove the President Had Nothing to Hide

Richard M. Nixon

On January 17, 1973, former Nixon aides G. Gordon Liddy and James W. McCord and three others were convicted of conspiracy, burglary, and wiretapping of the offices of the Democratic National Committee at the Watergate complex in Washington, D.C. Though President Richard M. Nixon distanced himself from these men and other advisers and members of his staff, and claimed that he had no knowledge of the break-in, between January and October 1973 evidence pointing to presidential misconduct began to surface in the *Washington Post*, the *New York Times*, and various news agency reports. The most damaging piece of evidence to date was a letter from McCord to Judge John J. Sirica claiming that the defendants had pleaded guilty under pressure from Nixon's attorney John Dean and Attorney General John Mitchell, and that McCord committed perjury at his trial.

McCord's accusations that the White House knew of the burglary and the attempt to cover it up spurred investigators to intensify their search for evidence. When former White House aide Alexander P. Butterfield told investigators that Nixon routinely taped all his Oval Office conversations and meetings using a secret taping system, the search naturally turned to those tape transcripts. The House Judiciary Committee requested that Nixon turn over the tapes for examination, a request that he flatly refused. After months of ignored requests, then selective compliance regarding certain tapes, Nixon decided to turn over edited transcripts of the remaining

Richard M. Nixon, address to the nation, Washington, DC, April 29, 1974.

taped conversations. In the following excerpt from his speech to the nation, broadcast on April 29, 1974, Nixon explains his decision to release transcripts instead of the actual tapes. He maintains that sensitive and classified information on issues of national security is contained on the recordings, and thus that it would be a violation of executive privilege to release the tapes to the investigating committee.

I have asked for this time tonight in order to announce my answer to the House Judiciary Committee's subpoena for additional Watergate tapes, and to tell you something about the actions I shall be taking tomorrow—about what I hope they will mean to you and about the very difficult choices that were presented to me.

These actions will at last, once and for all, show that what I knew and what I did with regard to the Watergate break-in and coverup were just as I have described them to you from the very beginning.

I have spent many hours during the past few weeks thinking about what I would say to the American people if I were to reach the decision I shall announce tonight. And so, my words have not been lightly chosen; I can assure you they are deeply felt.

Nixon Cooperates with Investigators

It was almost 2 years ago, in June 1972 that five men broke into the Democratic National Committee headquarters in Washington. It turned out that they were connected with my reelection committee, and the Watergate break-in became a major issue in the campaign.

The full resources of the FBI and the Justice Department were used to investigate the incident thoroughly. I instructed my staff and campaign aides to cooperate fully with the investigation. The FBI conducted nearly 1,500 interviews. For 9 months—until March 1973—I was assured by those charged with conducting and monitoring the investigations that no one in the White House was involved.

Nevertheless, for more than a year, there have been allegations and insinuations that I knew about the planning of the Watergate break-in and that I was involved in an extensive plot to cover it up. The House Judiciary Committee is now investigating these charges.

On March 6, I ordered all materials that I had previously furnished to the Special Prosecutor turned over to the committee. These included tape recordings of 19 Presidential conversations and more than 700 documents from private White House files.

On April 11, the Judiciary Committee issued a subpoena for 42 additional tapes of conversations which it contended were necessary for its investigation. I agreed to respond to that subpoena by tomorrow.

Turning Over Transcripts Instead of Tapes

In these folders that you see over here on my left are more than 1,200 pages of transcripts of private conversations I participated in between September 15, 1972, and April 27 of 1973 with my principal aides and associates with regard to Watergate. They include all the relevant portions of all of the subpoenaed conversations that were recorded, that is, all portions that relate to the question of what I knew about Watergate or the coverup and what I did about it.

They also include transcripts of other conversations which were not subpoenaed, but which have a significant bearing on the question of Presidential actions with regard to Watergate. These will be delivered to the committee tomorrow.

In these transcripts, portions not relevant to my knowledge or actions with regard to Watergate are not included, but everything that is relevant is included—the rough as well as the smooth—the strategy sessions, the exploration of alternatives, the weighing of human and political costs.

As far as what the President personally knew and did with regard to Watergate and the coverup is concerned, these materials—together with those already made available—will tell it all.

I shall invite Chairman [Peter] Rodino and the committee's ranking minority member, Congressman [Edward] Hutchinson of Michigan, to come to the White House and listen to the actual, full tapes of these conversations, so that they can determine for themselves beyond question that the transcripts are accurate and that everything on the tapes relevant to my knowledge and my actions on Watergate is included. If there should be any disagreement over whether omitted material is relevant, I shall meet with them personally in an effort to settle the matter. I believe this arrangement is fair, and I think it is appropriate.

For many days now, I have spent many hours of my own time personally reviewing these materials and personally deciding questions of relevancy. I believe it is appropriate that the committee's review should also be made by its own senior elected officials, and not by staff employees. . . .

The Issue of Executive Privilege

But the problem I confronted was this: Unless a President can protect the privacy of the advice he gets, he cannot get the advice he needs.

This principle is recognized in the constitutional doctrine of executive privilege, which has been defended and maintained by every President since Washington and which has been recognized by the courts, whenever tested, as inherent in the Presidency. I consider it to be my constitutional responsibility to defend this principle.

Three factors have now combined to persuade me that a major unprecedented exception to that principle is now necessary:

First, in the present circumstances, the House of Representatives must be able to reach an informed judgment about the President's role in Watergate.

I want there to be no question remaining about the fact that the President has nothing to hide in this matter.

Second, I am making a major exception to the principle of confidentiality because I believe such action is now necessary in order to restore the principle itself, by clearing the air of the central question that has brought such pressures upon it—and also to provide the evidence which will allow this matter to be brought to a prompt conclusion.

Third, in the context of the current impeachment climate, I believe all the American people, as well as their representatives in Congress, are entitled to have not only the facts but also the evidence that demonstrates those facts.

I want there to be no question remaining about the fact that the President has nothing to hide in this matter.

The impeachment of a President is a remedy of last resort; it is the most solemn act of our entire constitutional process. Now, regardless of whether or not it succeeded, the action of the House, in voting a formal accusation requiring trial by the Senate, would put the Nation through a wrenching ordeal it has endured only once in its lifetime, a century ago, and never since America has become a world power with global responsibilities.

The impact of such an ordeal would be felt throughout the world, and it would have its effect on the lives of all Americans for many years to come.

Because this is an issue that profoundly affects all the American people, in addition to turning over these transcripts to the House Judiciary Committee, I have directed that they should all be made public—all of these that you see here.

And I was also concerned about the human impact on others, especially some of the young people . . . whose lives might be suddenly ruined by something they had done in an excess of loyalty.

To complete the record, I shall also release to the public transcripts of all those portions of the tapes already turned over to the Special Prosecutor and to the committee that relate to Presidential actions or knowledge of the Watergate affair. . . .

I have been reluctant to release these tapes, not just because they will embarrass me and those with whom I have talked—which they will—and not just because they will become the subject of speculation and even ridicule—which they will—and not just because certain parts of them will be seized upon by political and journalistic opponents—which they will.

I have been reluctant because, in these and in all the other conversations in this office, people have spoken their minds freely, never dreaming that specific sentences or even parts of sentences would be picked out as the subjects of national attention and controversy.

I have been reluctant because the principle of confidentiality is absolutely essential to the conduct of the Presidency. In reading the raw transcripts of these conversations, I believe it will be more readily apparent why that principle is essential and must be maintained in the future. These conversations are unusual in their subject matter, but the same kind of uninhibited discussion—and it is that—the same brutal candor is necessary in discussing how to bring warring factions to the peace table or how to move necessary legislation through the Congress.

Names are named in these transcripts. Therefore, it is important to remember that much that appears in them is no more than hearsay or speculation, exchanged as I was trying to find out what really had happened, while my principal aides were reporting to me on rumors and reports that they had heard, while we discussed the various, often conflicting stories that different persons were telling.

Transcripts Will Reveal Nixon's Innocence

As the transcripts will demonstrate, my concerns during this period covered a wide range. The first and obvious one was to find out just exactly what had happened and who was involved.

A second concern was for the people who had been, or might become, involved in Watergate. Some were close advisers, valued friends, others whom I had trusted. And I was also concerned about the human impact on others, especially some of the young people and their families who had come to Washington to work in my Administration, whose lives might be suddenly ruined by something they had done in an excess of loyalty or in the mistaken belief that it would serve the interests of the President.

And then, I was quite frankly concerned about the political implications. This represented potentially a devastating blow to the Administration and to its programs, one which I knew would be exploited for all it was worth by hostile elements in the Congress as well as in the media. I wanted to do what was right, but I wanted to do it in a way that would cause the least unnecessary damage in a highly charged political atmosphere to the Administration.

And fourth, as a lawyer, I felt very strongly that I had to conduct myself in a way that would not prejudice the rights of potential defendants.

And fifth, I was striving to sort out a complex tangle, not

only of facts but also questions of legal and moral responsibility. I wanted, above all, to be fair. I wanted to draw distinctions, where those were appropriate, between persons who were active and willing participants on the one hand, and on the other, those who might have gotten inadvertently caught up in the web and be technically indictable but morally innocent.

Despite the confusions and contradictions, what does come through clearly is this:

[Nixon aide] John Dean charged in sworn Senate testimony that I was "fully aware of the coverup" at the time of our first meeting on September 15, 1972. These transcripts show clearly that I first learned of it when Mr. Dean himself told me about it in this office on March 21—some 6 months later.

Incidentally, these transcripts—covering hours upon hours of conversations—should place in somewhat better perspective the controversy over the 18½ minute gap in the tape of a conversation I had with Mr. [H.R.] Haldeman [White House Chief-of-Staff] back in June of 1972.

Now, how it was caused is still a mystery to me and, I think, to many of the experts as well. But I am absolutely certain, however, of one thing: that it was not caused intentionally by my secretary, Rose Mary Woods, or any of my White House assistants. And certainly, if the theory were true that during those 18½ minutes, Mr. Haldeman and I cooked up some sort of a Watergate coverup scheme, as so many have been quick to surmise, it hardly seems likely that in all of our subsequent conversations—many of them are here—which neither of us ever expected would see the light of day, there is nothing remotely indicating such a scheme; indeed, quite the contrary.

From the beginning, I have said that in many places on the tapes there were ambiguities—a statement and comments that different people with different perspectives might interpret in drastically different ways—but although the words may be ambiguous, though the discussions may have explored many alternatives, the record of my actions is totally clear now, and I still believe it was totally correct then.

4

Nixon's Refusal to Cooperate Implicates Him in Criminal Activity

Washington Post

In May 1974, a year after the Watergate incident took on the proportions of a national scandal, President Richard Nixon decided to end White House cooperation with the investigation of his possible involvement with the break-in, including the independent counsel Leon Jaworski and the House Judiciary Committee. Nixon asserted that the committee and the independent counsel's office had sufficient evidence to proceed with a hearing and refused to turn over any further transcripts or audiotapes of secret White House conversations. The following editorial in the *Washington Post*, the newspaper that was primarily responsible for breaking the Watergate story and keeping Watergate in the public eye, argues that Nixon's refusal to cooperate is not only incriminating but also unconstitutional. The editors consider Nixon's act grounds for impeachment. Finally, they call for the hearings into his involvement to continue regardless of any further cooperation by the Nixon administration.

The president has an odd way of celebrating Watergate anniversaries. Yesterday marked the passage of one full year since Mr. [Richard M.] Nixon issued his compendious statement of May 22, 1973, promising to make available all revelant information on the complex of scandals that go by the name of Watergate. He chose to commemorate the occasion by informing the House Judiciary Committee, which is conducting impeachment hearings and which has—if anything—a larger and stronger claim on relevant evidence than the other bodies of inquiry do, that he would decline to produce any further Watergate tapes requested or subpoenaed by it. The full story of Watergate and of his own involvment in it, Mr. Nixon advised the committee, reposes in the White House materials already in the committee's hands.

In more ways than one, that is an interesting assertion. It not only confirms that the President is prepared to defy the committee's requests for material it deems necessary to conducting its inquiry. It also confirms that there is no better documentary case for Mr. Nixon to make concerning his own role in the coverup than that which can be made (if it can) from the highly incriminating documents and tapes now in the committee's possession. May 22, 1974, was a bleak day for those who still held out hope that somewhere, somehow, the President could come forward with persuasive exculpatory evidence. Apparently there is none.

Enough Evidence Exists to Implicate Nixon

Although we believe that Mr. Nixon's outright defiance of Congress in this matter is as unconstitutional as it is unwise, it does occur to us that he has a point in his assertion that more than enough is now known for the committee to act— never mind that it isn't the point he was seeking to make. For the plain fact is that both the magnitude of the shocks and revelations of the past year and the complicated legal disputes the President has promoted and prolonged with Congress and the courts have combined to distract people from what they already know. They have given the whole sorry affair the aspect of a continuing, if not interminable, Grade B thriller, as distinct from the aspect of a body of confirmed information which is, in itself, more than sufficient to require a public response. The question, in other words, is not so much "what is going to happen next?" or "what will we learn about tomorrow?" but, rather, "what do we already know?"

Think about it: we know plenty.

We know that the President's best defense throughout—and it is a terrible defense—is that he so mismanaged the conduct of his office that he was unaware that his aides were authorizing common burglaries, were forging State Department cables, were perjuring themselves before federal prosecutors and grand juries, were paying blackmail money to criminals to buy silence about the White House's own involvement in their crimes, were systematically seeking to politicize and pervert the allegedly apolitical agencies of government (the CIA, the IRS, the FBI, among others) for the sake of wreaking personal vengeance on institutions and individuals they considered enemies.

[Nixon] is only doing these recalcitrant things to protect "future" presidents. We think the evidence is overwhelming that he is, on the contrary, trying only to protect this one.

We know that the President on the eve of the sentencing of the originally convicted Watergate conspirators, learned that their trial had been skewed by perjured testimony and failed to so inform the judge.

We know that the President has repeatedly and systematically misled the American public in his statements "from the heart" on this matter, telling them things he knew to be untrue.

We know that six of his former aides have been sentenced to terms in federal penitentiaries.

We know that his appointees have conspired to destroy evidence in criminal cases.

We know that the man he twice selected to be his (and our) Vice President has been convicted of a felony, forced to resign office and disbarred from the practice of law.

We know that the President—a great scourge of "welfare cheating"—was found to be almost half a million dollars light on his federal income tax.

We know that indictments are now outstanding and trials awaited for his closest White House associates and one-time most powerful deputies for a series of alleged criminal acts. We know that he has, while claiming all the protections and safeguards accorded an ordinary citizen in trouble with the law, simultaneously and shamelessly utilized the great and unique powers of the presidency not only to argue his own case (falsely) but to protect himself from scrutiny by the Congress or the courts. He declines to honor subpoenas. He fires the Special Prosecutor he has promised to give full rein when that Prosecutor appears to be getting warm. And now he tells us, in the course of telling the House Judiciary Committee, that he is only doing these recalcitrant things to protect "future" presidents. We think the evidence is overwhelming that he is, on the contrary, trying only to protect this one.

Congress Must Push the Investigation Forward

Presumably the members of the House Judiciary Committee and those legislators outside the committee who have authorized its inquiry will seek some further action on the materials Mr. Nixon has now declined to furnish. And presumably, too, his defiance of the committee will be added to the list of Constitution-bending offenses for which he, as President, is responsible. But we would hope that the committee would not permit itself to be drawn into a prolonged and diverting dispute over the production of this evidence to the exclusion of its responsibility to continue and conclude its inquiry as quickly and carefully as possible. The American people know plenty—and the members of the Judiciary Committee know even more. A variety of charges against Mr. [Vice President Spiro] Agnew were never fully adjudicated because he preferred that they not be, and the same may be true of certain of the charges against Mr. Nixon because he too has now indicated that he will not risk orderly and complete adjudication in a single body that is empowered to consider his case—namely, the United States Congress. Mr. Agnew copped a plea. Mr. Nixon is merely refusing, in the name of his office—or what remains of it—to let the full information come to light.

People have been, in our view, exceptionally patient so far, and that is especially true of the legislators themselves. And they have also been exceptionally judicious and restrained. But it seems to us that by this latest act of evasion and contempt, the President has released everyone from the injunction against drawing inferences from his refusal to produce subpoenaed evidence. And if he will not cooperate—so be it: the House will have to proceed without him on the basis of what it now knows.

5

The President Should Be Impeached

House Judiciary Committee

On July 27, 1974, in light of convincing evidence pointing to Nixon's conspiracy in criminal activity, the House Judiciary Committee voted 21-17 to pass a final draft of impeachment articles, the first step in removing a president from office. On August 5, the embattled Nixon released tapes showing that indeed he had participated in the Watergate cover-up as early as June 23, 1972, a direct contradiction of his previous statements. His supporters in Congress expressed shock and a sense of betrayal; it seemed clear that the House of Representatives would impeach him and that the Senate would convict him. On August 8 Nixon announced, without admitting guilt, that he would resign the presidency. He did so the following day, and Vice President Gerald Ford was immediately sworn in as his successor. Because he resigned, Nixon never faced an impeachment trial and the articles were never formally voted upon by Congress.

Impeaching Richard M. Nixon, President of the United States, of high crimes and misdemeanors.

Resolved, that Richard M. Nixon, President of the United States, is impeached for high crimes and misdemeanors, and that the following articles of impeachment be exhibited to the Senate:

Articles of impeachment exhibited by the House of Representatives of the United States of America in the name of

House Judiciary Committee, "Articles of Impeachment," July 27, 1974.

itself and of all of the people of the United States of America, against Richard M. Nixon, President of the United States of America, in maintenance and support of its impeachment against him for high crimes and misdemeanors.

Article I: Participation in the Cover-Up Scandal

In his conduct of the office of President of the United States, Richard M. Nixon, in violation of his constitutional oath faithfully to execute the office of President of the United States, and, to the best of his ability, preserve, protect, and defend the Constitution of the United States, and in violation of his constitutional duty to take care that the laws be faithfully executed, has prevented, obstructed, and impeded the administration of justice, in that:

On June 17, 1972, and prior thereto, agents of the Committee for the Re-election of the President committed unlawful entry of the headquarters of the Democratic National Committee in Washington, District of Columbia, for the purpose of securing political intelligence. Subsequent thereto, Richard M. Nixon, using the powers of his high office, engaged personally and through his subordinates and agents, in a course of conduct or plan designed to delay, impede, and obstruct the investigation of such unlawful entry, to cover up, conceal, and protect those responsible, and to conceal the existence and scope of other unlawful covert activities.

The means used to implement this course of conduct or plan included one or more of the following:

(1) making or causing to be made false or misleading statements to lawfully authorized investigative officers and employees of the United States;

(2) withholding relevant and material evidence or information from lawfully authorized investigative officers and employees of the United States;

(3) approving, condoning, acquiescing in, and counseling witnesses with respect to the giving of false or misleading statements to lawfully authorized investigative officers and employees of the United States and false or misleading testimony in duly instituted judicial and congressional proceedings;

(4) interfering or endeavoring to interfere with the conduct of investigations by the Department of Justice of the

United States, the Federal Bureau of Investigation, the Office of Watergate Special Prosecution Force, and Congressional Committees;

(5) approving, condoning, and acquiescing in the surreptitious payment of substantial sums of money for the purpose of obtaining the silence or influencing the testimony of witnesses, potential witnesses, or individuals who participated in such unlawful entry and other illegal activities;

(6) endeavoring to misuse the Central Intelligence Agency, an agency of the United States;

(7) disseminating information received from officers of the Department of Justice of the United States to subjects of investigations conducted by lawfully authorized investigative officers and employees of the United States, for the purpose of aiding and assisting such subjects in their attempts to avoid criminal liability;

(8) making false or misleading public statements for the purpose of deceiving the people of the United States into believing that a thorough and complete investigation had been conducted with respect to allegations of misconduct on the part of personnel of the executive branch of the United States and personnel of the Committee for the Re-election of the President, and that there was no involvement of such personnel in such misconduct; or

(9) endeavoring to cause prospective defendants, and individuals duly tried and convicted, to expect favored treatment and consideration in return for their silence or false testimony, or rewarding individuals for their silence or false testimony.

In all of this, Richard M. Nixon has acted in a manner contrary to his trust as President and subversive of constitutional government, to the great prejudice of the cause of law and justice and to the manifest injury of the people of the United States.

Wherefore, Richard M. Nixon, by such conduct, warrants impeachment and trial, and removal from office.

Article II: Abuse of Presidential Powers

Using the powers of the office of President of the United States, Richard M. Nixon, in violation of his constitutional oath faithfully to execute the office of President of the United States and, to the best of his ability, preserve, protect, and defend the Constitution of the United States, and in disregard of his constitutional duty to take care that the laws be faithfully executed, has repeatedly engaged in conduct violating the constitutional rights of citizens, impairing the due and proper administration of justice and the conduct of lawful inquiries, or contravening the laws governing agencies of the executive branch and the purposes of these agencies.

In all of this, Richard M. Nixon has acted in a manner contrary to his trust as President . . . to the great prejudice of the cause of law and justice and to the manifest injury of the people of the United States.

This conduct has included one or more of the following:

(1) He has, acting personally and through his subordinates and agents, endeavored to obtain from the Internal Revenue Service, in violation of the constitutional rights of citizens, confidential information contained in income tax returns for purposes not authorized by law, and to cause, in violation of the constitutional rights of citizens, income tax audits or other income tax investigations to be initiated or conducted in a discriminatory manner.

(2) He misused the Federal Bureau of Investigation, the Secret Service, and other executive personnel, in violation or disregard of the constitutional rights of citizens, by directing or authorizing such agencies or personnel to conduct or continue electronic surveillance or other investigations for purposes unrelated to national security, the enforcement of laws, or any other lawful function of his office; and he did direct the concealment of certain records made by the Federal Bureau of Investigation of electronic surveillance.

(3) He has, acting personally and through his subordinates and agents, in violation or disregard of the constitutional rights of citizens, authorized and permitted to be maintained a secret investigative unit within the office of the President, financed in part with money derived from campaign contributions, which unlawfully utilized the resources of the Central Intelligence Agency, engaged in covert and unlawful activities, and attempted to prejudice

the constitutional right of an accused to a fair trial.

(4) He has failed to take care that the laws were faithfully executed by failing to act when he knew or had reason to know that his close subordinates endeavored to impede and frustrate lawful inquiries by duly constituted executive, judicial, and legislative entities concerning the unlawful entry into the headquarters of the Democratic National Committee, and the cover-up thereof, and concerning other unlawful activities, including those relating to the confirmation of Richard Kleindienst as Attorney General of the United States, the electronic surveillance of private citizens, the break-in into the offices of Dr. Lewis Fielding, and the campaign financing practices of the Committee to Re-elect the President.

(5) In disregard of the rule of law, he knowingly misused the executive power by interfering with agencies of the executive branch, including the Federal Bureau of Investigation, the Criminal Division, and the Office of Watergate Special Prosecution Force, of the Department of Justice, and the Central Intelligence Agency, in violation of his duty to take care that the laws be faithfully executed.

Richard M. Nixon, by such conduct, warrants impeachment and trial, and removal from office.

In all of this, Richard M. Nixon has acted in a manner contrary to his trust as President and subversive of constitutional government, to the great prejudice of the cause of law and justice and to the manifest injury of the people of the United States.

Wherefore Richard M. Nixon, by such conduct, warrants impeachment and trial, and removal from office.

Article III: Failure to Cooperate with Investigators

In his conduct of the office of President of the United States, Richard M. Nixon, contrary to his oath faithfully to execute the office of President of the United States and, to the best of his ability, preserve, protect, and defend the Constitution of the United States, and in violation of his constitutional duty to take care that the laws be faithfully executed, has failed without lawful cause or excuse to produce papers and things as directed by duly authorized subpoenas issued by the Committee on the Judiciary of the House of Representatives on April 11, 1974, May 15, 1974, May 30, 1974, and June 24, 1974, and willfully disobeyed such subpoenas. The subpoenaed papers and things were deemed necessary by the Committee in order to resolve by direct evidence fundamental, factual questions relating to Presidential direction, knowledge, or approval of actions demonstrated by other evidence to be substantial grounds for impeachment of the President. In refusing to produce these papers and things, Richard M. Nixon, substituting his judgment as to what materials were necessary for the inquiry, interposed the powers of the Presidency against the lawful subpoenas of the House of Representatives, thereby assuming to himself functions and judgments necessary to the exercise of the sole power of impeachment vested by the Constitution in the House of Representatives.

In all of this, Richard M. Nixon has acted in a manner contrary to his trust as President and subversive of constitutional government, to the great prejudice of the cause of law and justice, and to the manifest injury of the people of the United States.

Wherefore Richard M. Nixon, by such conduct, warrants impeachment and trial, and removal from office.

Potential Criminal Activities in Other Arenas

Cambodia Bombing

In his conduct of the office of President of the United States, Richard M. Nixon, in violation of his constitutional oath faithfully to execute the office of President of the United States, and in disregard of his constitutional duty to take care that the laws be faithfully executed, on and subsequent to March 17, 1969, authorized, ordered, and ratified the concealment from the Congress of the facts and the submission to the Congress of false and misleading statements concerning the existence, scope, and nature of American bombing operations in Cambodia in derogation of the power of the Congress to declare war, to make appropriations, and to raise and support armies, and by such conduct warrants impeachment and trial and removal from office.

Emoluments and Income Taxes

In his conduct of the office of President of the United States, Richard M. Nixon, in violation of his constitutional oath faithfully to execute the office of the President of the United States, and, to the best of his ability, preserve, protect, and defend the Constitution of the United States and in violation of his constitutional duty to take care that the laws be faithfully executed, did receive emoluments from the United States in excess of the compensation provided by law pursuant to Article II, Section 1, Clause 7 of the Constitution, and did willfully attempt to evade the payment of Federal income taxes due and owing by him for the years 1969, 1970, 1971, and 1972, in that

(1) He, during the period for which he has been elected President, unlawfully received compensation in the form of government expenditures at and on his privately owned properties located in or near San Clemente, California, and Key Biscayne, Florida.

(2) He knowingly and fraudulently failed to report certain income and claimed deductions in the year 1969, 1970, 1971, and 1972 on his Federal income tax returns which were not authorized by law, including deductions for a gift of papers to the United States valued at approximately $576,000.

In all of this, Richard M. Nixon has acted in a manner contrary to his trust as President and subversive of constitutional government, to the great prejudice of the cause of law and justice and to the manifest injury of the people of the United States.

Wherefore Richard M. Nixon, by such conduct, warrants impeachment and trial, and removal from office.

6

Nixon Should
Be Pardoned

Gerald R. Ford

Facing certain impeachment and possible indictment and trial for his role in the Watergate conspiracy, Richard Nixon resigned the presidency on August 8, 1974. The scandal had consumed national attention for nearly two years and it was believed a Nixon trial might not begin for as much as another year. His successor, Gerald R. Ford, therefore decided that the nation's best interests would be served by granting Nixon a full pardon for any and all offenses connected to Watergate. He announced this controversial decision in a televised address to the nation on September 8, 1974, stating his beliefs that this chapter in U.S. history should be closed as quickly as possible and that Nixon's resignation in disgrace from the country's highest elected office was punishment enough.

L adies and gentlemen:
    I have come to a decision which I felt I should tell you and all of my fellow American citizens, as soon as I was certain in my own mind and in my own conscience that it is the right thing to do. I have learned already in this office that the difficult decisions always come to this desk. I must admit that many of them do not look at all the same as the hypothetical questions that I have answered freely and perhaps too fast on previous occasions.

My customary policy is to try and get all the facts and to consider the opinions of my countrymen and to take coun-

Gerald R. Ford, televised address to the nation, Washington, DC, September 8, 1974.

sel with my most valued friends. But these seldom agree, and in the end, the decision is mine. To procrastinate, to agonize, and to wait for a more favorable turn of events that may never come or more compelling external pressures that may as well be wrong as right, is itself a decision of sorts and a weak and potentially dangerous course for a President to follow.

I have promised to uphold the Constitution, to do what is right as God gives me to see the right, and to do the very best that I can for America. I have asked your help and your prayers, not only when I became President but many times since. The Constitution is the supreme law of our land and it governs our actions as citizens. Only the laws of God, which govern our consciences, are superior to it.

As we are a nation under God, so I am sworn to uphold our laws with the help of God. And I have sought such guidance and searched my own conscience with special diligence to determine the right thing for me to do with respect to my predecessor in this place, Richard Nixon, and his loyal wife and family. Theirs is an American tragedy in which we all have played a part. It could go on and on and on, or someone must write the end to it. I have concluded that only I can do that, and if I can, I must.

Many months and perhaps more years will have to pass before Richard Nixon could obtain a fair trial by jury in any jurisdiction of the United States.

There are no historic or legal precedents to which I can turn in this matter, none that precisely fit the circumstances of a private citizen who has resigned the Presidency of the United States. But it is common knowledge that serious allegations and accusations hang like a sword over our former President's head, threatening his health as he tries to reshape his life, a great part of which was spent in the service of this country and by the mandate of its people.

After years of bitter controversy and divisive national debate, I have been advised, and I am compelled to conclude that many months and perhaps more years will have to pass before Richard Nixon could obtain a fair trial by jury in any jurisdiction of the United States under governing decisions of the Supreme Court.

I deeply believe in equal justice for all Americans, whatever their station or former station. The law, whether human or divine, is no respecter of persons; but the law is a respecter of reality.

The facts, as I see them, are that a former President of the United States, instead of enjoying equal treatment with any other citizen accused of violating the law, would be cruelly and excessively penalized either in preserving the presumption of his innocence or in obtaining a speedy determination of his guilt in order to repay a legal debt to society.

My conscience tells me that only I, as President, have the constitutional power to firmly shut and seal this book.

During this long period of delay and potential litigation, ugly passions would again be aroused. And our people would again be polarized in their opinions. And the credibility of our free institutions of government would again be challenged at home and abroad. In the end, the courts might well hold that Richard Nixon had been denied due process, and the verdict of history would even more be inconclusive with respect to those charges arising out of the period of his Presidency, of which I am presently aware.

But it is not the ultimate fate of Richard Nixon that most concerns me, though surely it deeply troubles every decent and every compassionate person. My concern is the immediate future of this great country. In this, I dare not depend upon my personal sympathy as a long-time friend of the former President, nor my professional judgment as a lawyer, and I do not.

As President, my primary concern must always be the greatest good of all the people of the United States whose servant I am. As a man, my first consideration is to be true to my own convictions and my own conscience.

My conscience tells me clearly and certainly that I cannot prolong the bad dreams that continue to reopen a chapter that is closed. My conscience tells me that only I, as President, have the constitutional power to firmly shut and seal this book. My conscience tells me it is my duty, not merely to proclaim domestic tranquillity but to use every means that I have to insure it.

I do believe that the buck stops here, that I cannot rely upon public opinion polls to tell me what is right.

I do believe that right makes might and that if I am wrong, 10 angels swearing I was right would make no difference.

I do believe, with all my heart and mind and spirit, that I, not as President but as a humble servant of God, will receive justice without mercy if I fail to show mercy.

Finally, I feel that Richard Nixon and his loved ones have suffered enough and will continue to suffer, no matter what I do, no matter what we, as a great and good nation, can do together to make his goal of peace come true.

[At this point, the President began reading from the proclamation granting the pardon.]

"Now, therefore, I, Gerald R. Ford, President of the United States, pursuant to the pardon power conferred upon me by Article II, Section 2, of the Constitution, have granted and by these presents do grant a full, free, and absolute pardon unto Richard Nixon for all offenses against the United States which he, Richard Nixon, has committed or may have committed or taken part in during the period from July [January] 20, 1969, through August 9, 1974."

[The President signed the proclamation and then resumed reading.]

"In witness whereof, I have hereunto set my hand this eighth day of September, in the year of our Lord nineteen hundred and seventy-four, and of the Independence of the United States of America the one hundred and ninety-ninth."

Chapter 2

The Role of the Media in the Watergate Crisis

1

The Media Played a Critical Role in Watergate

Gladys Engel Lang and Kurt Lang

Watergate was an example of market saturation in the media; that is, the media made it a significant story by covering it so exhaustively and relentlessly that broad public awareness was inevitable. At the height of the Watergate scandal, almost every newspaper, radio, and television outlet covered Watergate at the expense of other major news dealings such as the Vietnam War, the Strategic Arms Limitation Talks (SALT), and domestic unrest stemming from the antiwar movement. In the following excerpt from their book *The Battle for Public Opinion: The Press, the President, and the Polls During Watergate*, media research analysts Gladys Engel Lang and Kurt Lang discuss the issue of saturation coverage and its impact on the public's view of President Richard Nixon. The Langs contend that such prominent coverage—prime-time special reports, front-page headlines, gavel-to-gavel televised hearings— forced the public to pay attention and finally motivated public demands to get to the bottom of the Watergate scandal.

The Watergate story appeared to have been all but buried in the immediate 1972 post-election period. Was it the renewed attention the news media gave it the next spring that accounted for its emergence as an issue?

First, Watergate as a news story, even immediately after

the election, never altogether disappeared from sight. Things kept happening. In December 1972, when Dorothy Hunt, the wife of Watergate defendant H.L. Hunt, died in an airline crash in Chicago, her purse was discovered to contain a large sum of money, all in hundred-dollar bills. This brought Watergate briefly back into the headlines. Other Watergate news centered around Judge Sirica, whose court had jurisdiction over the trial of the defendants in the Watergate burglary case. In December, Sirica became involved in a dispute with the *Los Angeles Times* over its publication of an interview with a former FBI agent, Alfred Baldwin, who had been a member of the unit responsible for the Watergate break-in and a key witness in the upcoming trial. Then, through most of January, it was the trial itself that drew attention. When the defendants, over the objections of their own counsel, decided to change their plea to guilty on all counts, Sirica openly questioned their motives, noting that this would remove the accused permanently from all questioning in open court. A spate of stories in the press alleged that Hunt was behind the change, that the men were being paid for keeping silent by persons unnamed. These stories originated mainly in the *New York Times*, the *Washington Post*, *Time*, and in the syndicated columns of Jack Anderson. Judge Sirica, aware of these allegations, sharply questioned the defendants but could not shake them. All denied that they were being coerced in any shape, manner, or form, insisting that they were not being paid by anybody for anything. Sirica made it clear that he did not believe them, and at the end of the trial, on January 30, declared that the full facts behind the break-in had yet to be unearthed.

Watergate Buried Amidst National Events

By the big play it gave Sirica's suspicions and through editorial comment, an important part of the press was beginning to convert the story of Watergate from a "bungled burglary" into a "coverup" and a quest for the truth. For example, a January 13 editorial in the *New York Times* said the question in need of an answer was who had hired the defendants. It called for the appointment of a special and independent prosecutor. At issue, as the editorial put it, was the "integrity and credibility" of an administration that, for the next four years, had to be "accountable to the American people."

Soon, the Senate's first steps toward an investigation of

its own also made news. In early January, its Democratic caucus voted to ask Senator Sam Ervin, a North Carolina Democrat, to head a probe of the Watergate affair, a move Sirica supported by publicly hoping, on February 2, that the Senate committee would be granted sufficient power "to get to the bottom of what happened in this case." On February 7, the Senate, miffed at Nixon's failure to deliver his State of the Union message in person, unanimously adopted a resolution to establish a seven-man select committee to probe all aspects of the bugging case and other reported instances of attempted political espionage against the Democrats during the 1972 election campaign.

At issue . . . was the "integrity" and "credibility" of an administration that, for the next four years, had to be "accountable to the American people."

In January and February, these and other Watergate items often made newspaper headlines as well as the network news on television. Yet they were to be overshadowed by dramatic events that underlined Nixon's role as President and world leader. On January 20 he was inaugurated for his second term. The ceremonies, estimated to cost more than four million dollars, were more expensive than any previous American inaugural. "We stand," the President told the nation in his televised address, "on the threshold of a new era of peace in the world." Three days later, in a nationwide television report, the President announced that Henry Kissinger and the chief North Vietnamese negotiator, Le Duc Tho, had initialed an agreement "to end the war and bring peace with honor in Vietnam and Southeast Asia."

The release of Americans held prisoner in Vietnam began on February 12. With the arrival of the first group of men at Clark Air Force base in the Phillipines, it became a national television production. The first man out of the plane paid homage to home and country and, also, to Richard Nixon. "We are," said Navy Captain Jeremiah P. Denton, "profoundly grateful to our Commander-in-Chief." Air Force Colonel James Kasler was even more explicit, sounding a theme that Nixon would make very much his own. "President Nixon," he said, "has brought us home with honor."

During February and most of March Watergate developments also competed with other big stories. In February there was the devaluation of the dollar by 10 percent, then a continuing dollar crisis, which worsened in March and temporarily closed foreign exchange markets in Europe and Japan. Of less personal concern to most of the public but more sensational and good news copy was a 37-day confrontation between militant Indian leaders and federal troops around the Oglala Sioux hamlet of Wounded Knee, South Dakota. When the last POWs did come home late in March, the President again went on the air to announce that "for the first time in twelve years no American military forces are in Vietnam" but, by that time, developments in the Watergate story were dominating the news.

Watergate Returns to National Prominence

If Watergate never completely disappeared from view after the election, it was only in March that levels of coverage once again reached those of the previous fall and soon surpassed them. After late March time and space devoted to Watergate rose rapidly. By May the *New York Times* was carrying an average of 14 items a day, nearly eight times the average of the previous October and coverage in other major newspapers rose correspondingly. The increase in television coverage was even more dramatic, considering the time strictures of the network newscast. In the two weeks before the televised Senate hearings began, between 20 and 25 percent of the roughly 20 minutes available for hard news on the typical program was devoted to Watergate items.

This expanded coverage was not simply an increase in amount, but a change in kind. It marked the onset of the sort of *saturation* coverage that had been devoted to Watergate for only brief intervals in 1972. Saturation is the combined effect of *prominence* with *continuity:* Prominence, as operationalized here, means placement on the front page of a newspaper or devoting at least 60 seconds to an item on television; continuity requires such prominence on at least four out of five successive weekday telecasts or, in the case of newspapers (where one must make allowance for Sunday and Monday doldrums in the news) on four successive days, or five out of seven, or six out of nine. In no case can there be a break in front-page placement for longer than three days.

Prominence gives a news item the visibility that facilitates one's attention. Continuity allows for the kind of reiteration and development of news angles that help to fix the basic elements of a story in one's mind. Both are conducive to the emergence of an issue. Both are necessary before a high threshold event like Watergate can break through the barrier of public inattention to become a dominant concern. How much prominence and continuity are necessary to move an issue onto the public agenda depends on the political context. . . .

Watergate would have to be dealt with. What still remained unsettled was how the issue would be eventually resolved.

Through most of the 1972 campaign, whenever a network or a newspaper gave prominent and continuous coverage to Watergate, as several did from time to time, it tended to be alone in this. Most of the big Watergate stories in this period were developed by investigative reporters flushing out information the Nixon camp had been eager to hide. Competing newspapers and management were not always eager to feature what they themselves had not developed, and many of the exposés derived their news value from being tied to a specific deadline. This helps explain why even in October 1972, when all three networks gave saturation treatment to essentially the same events, the items were broadcast on different days. CBS was "Watergate-saturated" from October 13 through November 1, ABC from October 3 through 12, and NBC from October 13 through 25. The only Watergate-related development to receive saturation coverage simultaneously from at least two networks and the *New York Times* was the controversy in late August over the release of a report by the GAO [General Accounting Office] on illegal campaign contributions.

Trial of Watergate Defendants Increases News Coverage

In 1973 the pattern changed. The media ceased in any sense to act as prime movers on Watergate. Breaking stories not initiated by the press mandated timely coverage so that periods of saturation coverage began to more nearly overlap. What first breathed new life into the story was the start of the trial of the Watergate defendants, held in Washington with its unique concentration of news staffs. For much of January it provided a continuous flow of news. Other developments were the confirmation hearings of Patrick Gray as FBI director and the civil suits by attorneys of Nixon's re-election committee against 14 members of the press. But the real breakthrough did not come until March 23, the day before the Watergate defendants were to be sentenced. A letter by James McCord, one of the seven defendants, was read by Judge Sirica in open court. A bombshell, it spoke of "political pressure" on all the defendants to remain silent, of perjury during the trial, of higher-ups—not named—who were implicated in the Watergate operation. From this point on, the disclosures began to fit together. They had too much plausibility to be dismissed and calls for a detailed explanation from the Administration came from both politicians and journalists. The possibility that a major scandal was brewing could no longer be ignored, even by the regional press, many of whose editors and publishers had been and remained strong believers in the President.

Prominence gives a news item the visibility that facilitates one's attention.

The number of Watergate headlines briefly declined in early April. But after this hiatus, every one of five major newspapers we examined gave prominent coverage to every development for the entire month before the Senate hearings began. From mid-April through mid-May, 56 percent of the evening newscasts (on 23 weekdays) led off with a Watergate story. With Watergate generating so many damaging stories, the White House could no longer afford to appear unresponsive to demands that the President do something to clear up suspicions, especially since these demands also came from Republicans concerned about their political futures. Events were moving so fast that the White House, previously reluctant to comment on the subject, itself became an important generator of Watergate news.

One by one persons close to the Oval Office began to

be implicated. As news of McCord's testimony before the Watergate grand jury leaked out, the earlier Nixon strategy of diverting attention to other national issues no longer sufficed. The President finally (April 17) went on the offensive with two dramatic announcements of his own: first, he had initiated a "new inquiry" into the Watergate case leading to "major developments . . . concerning which it would be improper to be more specific"; second, in a partial retreat from a prior stand, he would permit testimony by White House aides before the Senate select committee under certain conditions. In adding that none of those who testified should expect immunity from prosecution, Nixon was talking as much to [Nixon aid and special counsel to the president] John Dean as to his own critics. He meant to cast Dean, whose lawyers were seeking such immunity in exchange for his testimony, in an unfavorable light as someone trying to shield himself from the consequences of past wrongdoing.

This effort failed to divert the media from pursuing the Watergate story. If anything it stirred interest in the newly developing controversy between the President and the Senate committee about the extent of its investigatory authority. Senator Sam Ervin, its chairman, made the front page when he insisted his Committee alone would be the final judge on whether White House aides could or could not refuse to answer questions. Ronald Ziegler, Nixon's press secretary, made equally big news when (April 17), after relaying Nixon's statement about "major new developments," he referred to all past statements about White House non-involvement as "inoperative." Incidentally, this phrase, which quickly became part of the expanding Watergate vocabulary, was not altogether Ziegler's invention but practically put into his mouth by reporters who had been badgering him to tell why the President was backtracking on his old insistence that no one in the White House had been implicated. Ziegler repeatedly avoided an answer by assuring them that "the president's statement today" is the "operative" statement. Finally, someone asked whether he was then saying that "the other statement . . . is *inoperative.*" "Yes," Ziegler replied, making Watergate history.

Press Stories Highlight Significant Events

The rash of resignations by persons high up in the Nixon administration, all duly reported by the press, told its own story. Then, on April 30, the White House announced the resignations of Nixon's two closest aides, John Erhlichman and H.R. Haldeman, along with those of Attorney General Richard Kleindienst and White House counsel John Dean. That evening, in a televised address, Nixon accepted responsibility for "those whose zeal exceeded their judgment" while denying any complicity either in the break-in or any attempt to cover up. He now conceded, that "there had been an effort to conceal the facts." In pointing out that in 1972 he had not, for the first time in his long political career, run his own political campaign, he suggested not only that he had been unaware of what CRP had been up to, but also that his own investigators had lied to him. From here on, he would leave Watergate to his new Attorney General, Elliott Richardson. Then, in a somewhat emotional appeal, he expressed his desire to be free of Watergate so he could spend his remaining 1361 days in office dealing with grave foreign and domestic matters.

Again, despite the President's attempt to put Watergate behind him, sometimes dramatic developments compelled more news coverage. One bombshell was the dismissal on May 11 of government charges of espionage, theft, and conspiracy against Daniel Ellsberg and Anthony J. Russo Jr., defendants in the Pentagon Papers trial, which ended abruptly because of an "unprecedented series of actions" by a special unit established in the White House. The reference was to a surreptitious entry into the office of Ellsberg's psychiatrist in search of confidential medical records to be used, as it later turned out, to discredit his patient politically. The opening of the televised Watergate hearings, on May 17, and the appointment, on May 18, of Archibald Cox as Special Watergate Prosecutor, placed the Watergate scandal and many things related to it on the agenda of several public bodies. Watergate would have to be dealt with. What still remained unsettled was how the issue would eventually be resolved.

The Public Conscience Made Watergate a Crisis

By Spring 1973 Watergate was on the *political* agenda. Congress had launched an investigation into illegal campaign practices. A newly appointed Special Prosecutor was given full authority to investigate and prosecute offenses arising out of the break-in to the Democratic National Headquarters and just about any other offenses relating to the election. By this time also, Watergate was on the *public* agenda. A significant segment of the citizenry was seriously concerned about the disclosures and wanted the government to do something, while opinion about the nature of the problem and what needed to be done was divided.

Politicians were becoming aware that as more and more people came to take Watergate seriously, most would react negatively to the appearance that anything was being covered up.

As yet, not many people saw in Watergate, as they would later, a personal threat to their own well-being, closely touching their lives. Public opinion four months into Nixon's second term could hardly be called "outraged," but neither could it be depicted any longer as "apathetic," as it had been as late as March. Gradually this public was making its presence felt. Politicians were becoming aware that as more and more people came to take Watergate seriously, most would react negatively to the appearance that anything was being covered up. Those in Congress pressing for a full investigation were able to ride the crest of this feeling. Public reaction to Nixon's April 30 speech supplied the ammunition they needed to outmaneuver those opposed to, or at least not enthusiastic about, a formal inquiry.

Watergate had broken into public consciousness only after the coverage had created a sense of crisis. This is not to say that the Watergate issue was something that the electronic and print media had created out of whole cloth. The coverage, which had stirred interest in Watergate, was dictated by events but the media themselves had become part of the field of action. Political figures with a stake in the outcome were using whatever publicity they could attract to advance their own goals and interests, thereby providing grist for the media and adding to the number of Watergate-relevant events there to be covered. As a result, the coverage reached saturation levels with Watergate on the front page and on the evening news day after day after day as well as on early morning, late evening, and Sunday public affairs programs. But the headlines alone would not have sufficed to make a serious issue out of a problem so removed from most people's daily concerns. Continuity was necessary to rivet attention to new facts as they emerged. The process is circular. Media exposure and public attention generate responses at the elite level that produce still more news in a cycle of mutual reinforcement that continues until politicians and public tire of an issue or another issue moves into the center of the political stage. . . .

None of this should be read to mean that the media, all on their own, dictate the public agenda. They cannot "teach" the public what the issues are. They certainly do not operate in total autonomy from the political system. The gradual saturation of news content with Watergate depended on political developments in which the press itself was only one of several movers. Agenda building—a more apt term than agenda setting—is a collective process in which media, government, and the citizenry reciprocally influence one another in at least some respects.

Factors in Setting a Media Agenda

Let us, in conclusion, sketch out how the news media affect this agenda-building process.

First, they highlight some events or activities. They make them stand out from among the myriads of other contemporaneous events and activities that could equally have been selected out for publicity. Making something the center of interest affects how much people will think and talk about it. This much is only common sense.

But, second, being in the news is not enough to guarantee attention to an issue. The amount and kind of coverage required varies from issue to issue. Different kinds of issues require different amounts and kinds of coverage to gain attention. Where news focuses on a familiar concern likely to affect almost everyone, this almost guarantees instant attention. In the case of a high-threshold issue like Watergate, which also surfaced at the wrong time, it takes saturation coverage to achieve this result. Specifically, recognition by the "cosmopolitan" media was not enough. Only after the more locally oriented press had become saturated with news of Watergate developments did it emerge as an issue that would remain on the political and public agenda for nearly 16 months.

Third, the events and activities in the focus of attention

still have to be framed, to be given a field of meanings within which they can be understood. They must come to stand for something, identify some problem, link up with some concern. The first exposé of the political fund used to finance the unit responsible for the break-in was publicized during a Presidential campaign. It was reported and interpreted within the context of that continuing contest. The Democrats' effort to change this context by interpreting Watergate as a symptom of widespread political corruption within the Administration was not very successful. Watergate remained, at least for a while, a partisan issue. The context had first to be changed.

Fourth, the language the media use to track events also affects the meaning imputed to them. Metaphors such as "Watergate caper" and "bugging incident," which belittled the issue, disappeared that spring under an avalanche of signs of a high-level political scandal. The press, along with politicians, adopted less deprecatory codewords. "Watergate" or "Watergate scandal" came to denote the various questionable activities now being disclosed. The words stood for nothing specific, yet for anything that could possibly happen.

Fifth, the media link the activities or events that have become the focus of attention to secondary symbols whose location on the political landscape is easily recognized. They also weave discrete events into a continuing political story, so that the lines of division on the issue as it develops tend to coincide with the cleavage between the organized political parties or between other sharply defined groups. The public is informed about what is the "Republican" or the "Democratic" position, or the position of any other group—for instance, producers vs. consumers, have vs. have-nots—so that potential partisans can align themselves. Often the lines of division around an issue about to surface are unclear. And they are likely to be fluid. When Watergate first surfaced during the 1972 campaign, it was defined primarily as a partisan clash between Democrats and Republicans. By Spring 1973 opinion still divided along political lines, but a realignment was under way as the issue changed and sides began to shape up around the "need to get the facts out," over the public "right to know" vs. "executive privilege," and on the question of confidence in the integrity of the government.

Finally, there are the prestige and standing of the spokes-men who articulate these concerns and demands. Their ef-fectiveness stems in good part from their ability to command media attention. Democratic politicians like Larry O'Brien and George McGovern had been lonely voices in the wilder-ness when, during the campaign, they pressed for a full in-vestigation. Their demands, though publicized, were neither much heard nor much heeded. They were known as people with an axe to grind. But as the controversy escalated, the publicity given Judge Sirica's admonishment that the full truth had not been told led prestigious Republicans to call for explanations, and their various attempts to get at the facts put pressure on the White House. The bystander public was being wooed.

The Media Bridges the Public to the Issue

The process of agenda-building, as we conceive of it, goes on continuously and involves several feedback loops. The most important of these are (1) the images through which politi-cal figures see themselves and their own activities mirrored in the media, (2) the pooling of information within the press corps that fosters similarities in the imagery disseminated, and (3) the various indicators of the public response, espe-cially opinion polling, towards which press and polity alike are oriented. As the controversy over Watergate continued, the nature of the issue continued to change, just as it had changed in the five months that followed the election.

As for the agenda-setting hypothesis: the media do play a vital role in calling attention to a problem, but neither public awareness nor public concern suffices to convert a problem into a public issue. It becomes a public issue only when the public can locate it on the political landscape and see reasons for taking sides. The news media help build these issues by establishing the necessary linkages between the polity and the public that facilitate the emergence of a problem as an issue. Once such linkages exist, even a high-threshold issue such as Watergate can retain its place on the public agenda against strong competition.

2

The *Washington Post's* Role in Watergate Has Been Exaggerated

Mark Feldstein

In June 1972 the *Washington Post* reported the Watergate break-in and followed the story until the November election, though few other newspapers picked up the story. By late 1972 *Post* reporters began to show connections between several of the Watergate burglars and White House staff members. By January 1973, enough evidence existed for the Senate to create a committee to investigate potential misconduct in the Nixon administration. The *Post* was by then joined by wide news coverage implicating the White House in the break-in, including reports in the *Los Angeles Times* and the *New York Times*. Critics of the *Washington Post* charge that *Post* reporters are given too much credit for exposing the scandal. In the following article from the *American Journalism Review*, for example, journalism professor Mark Feldstein contends that government investigation and carefully timed internal leaks, not the investigative brilliance of Carl Bernstein and Bob Woodward or the good judgment of the *Post's* editors and publisher, were the crucial factors in Nixon's downfall. Mark Feldstein is director of the journalism program in the School of Media and Public Affairs of George Washington University in Washington, D.C. He was previously an on-air network news correspondent for CNN, ABC News, and NBC News.

Thirty years ago, on August 9, 1974, the *Washington Post* ran what was then the largest front-page headline in its history: "Nixon Resigns."

That date marked both the end of Richard Nixon's presidency and the beginning of three decades of debate about what role journalism played in uncovering the Watergate scandal that forced Nixon from office—and how Watergate, in turn, influenced journalism itself. Did media muckraking actually bring down a president of the United States? How have politics and investigative reporting changed as a result?

Thirty years later, the answers to these basic questions remain nearly as polarized as they were in Nixon's day. While journalism schools continue to teach the lesson of Watergate as a heroic example of courageous press coverage under fire, some scholars have concluded that the media played at best a modest role in ousting Nixon from office. So what really happened? In the end, perhaps truth lies somewhere between the self-congratulatory boosterism of journalists and the kiss-off of the academics.

By now, of course, Watergate has become part of our folklore: Five men wearing business suits and surgical gloves arrested in the middle of the night with illegal bugging devices at the Democratic Party headquarters in the Watergate building in Washington, D.C. The burglars turned out to be part of a wide-ranging political espionage and sabotage operation run by President Nixon's top aides, one that triggered a massive White House cover-up directed by the president himself. After that cover-up unraveled, more than 70 people, including cabinet members and White House assistants, were convicted of criminal abuses of power; only a pardon by his presidential successor spared Nixon himself from becoming the first chief executive in history to be indicted for felonies committed in the Oval Office. In the words of [author] Stanley Kutler, the scandal's leading historian, Watergate "consumed and convulsed the nation and tested the constitutional and political system as it had not been tested since the Civil War."

The *Washington Post* Was Critical to Public Awareness of Watergate

As important as Watergate was in political history, it was perhaps equally so in journalism history. *Washington Post* reporters Bob Woodward and Carl Bernstein produced "the single most spectacular act of serious journalism [of the 20th] century," said media critic Ben Bagdikian. Marvin Kalb, a senior fellow at Harvard's Joan Shorenstein Center on the Press, Politics and Public Policy, believes that the *Post's* reporting was "absolutely critical" to "creating an atmosphere in Washington and within the government that Nixon was in serious trouble and that the White House was engaged in a cover-up. I believe that the reporting of Woodward and Bernstein represents a milestone of American journalism."

Journalism may have helped prepare the public ahead of time for Nixon's removal, . . . but it was Congress, not the media, that forced the president's resignation.

Even conservative critics have accepted the notion that Woodward and Bernstein were instrumental in Nixon's downfall. "[T]he *Washington Post* decided to make the Watergate break-in a major moral issue, a lead followed by the rest of the East Coast media," [author] Paul Johnson wrote in his book "Modern Times: A History of the World from the 1920s to the Year 2000." This "Watergate witch-hunt," Johnson declared, was "run by liberals in the media . . . the first media Putsch in history."

Woodward dismisses both detractors and fans who contend that the media unseated a president. "To say that the press brought down Nixon, that's horseshit," he says. "The press always plays a role, whether by being passive or by being aggressive, but it's a mistake to overemphasize" the media's coverage.

But it was Woodward and Bernstein's best-selling book, "All the President's Men," that focused public attention on the young reporters, especially after Hollywood turned it into a blockbuster movie starring [actors] Robert Redford and Dustin Hoffman. The film immortalized the chain-smoking anonymous source called "Deep Throat," who met Woodward at night in deserted parking garages after first signaling for meetings with elaborate codes. Warner Brothers promoted the movie as "the story of the two young reporters who cracked the Watergate conspiracy . . . [and] solved the greatest detective story in American history. At times, it looked as if it might cost them their jobs, their reputations, perhaps even their lives."

Despite the hype, Woodward and Bernstein did not write a comprehensive history of Watergate, just a memoir of their own experience covering it. "The fallacy in 'All the President's Men' is that the movie is all from our point of view, so that it seems to be a story about us," Woodward acknowledges. "But that's just one piece of what happened early in the process."

Still, as sociologist Michael Schudson wrote in his book "Watergate in American Memory," that's not the way the public sees it: "A mythology of the press in Watergate developed into a significant national myth, a story that independently carries on a memory of Watergate even as details about what Nixon did or did not do fade away. At its broadest, the myth of journalism in Watergate asserts that two young *Washington Post* reporters brought down the president of the United States. This is a myth of David and Goliath, of powerless individuals overturning an institution of overwhelming might. It is high noon in Washington, with two white-hatted young reporters at one end of the street and the black-hatted president at the other, protected by his minions. And the good guys win. The press, truth its only weapon, saves the day."

Some Critics View the Media's Role as Less Critical

How accurate is this scenario? Not very, according to Kutler, author of what is widely considered the most definitive history of the scandal, "The Wars of Watergate." "As more documentary materials are released," Kutler wrote, "the media's role in uncovering Watergate diminishes in scope and importance. Television and newspapers publicized the story and, perhaps, even encouraged more diligent investigation. But it is clear that as Watergate unfolded from 1972 to 1974, media revelations of crimes and political misdeeds repeated what was already known to properly constituted investigative authorities. In short, carefully timed leaks, not media investigations, provided the first news of Watergate."

"At best," wrote author Edward Jay Epstein, "reporters, including Woodward and Bernstein, only leaked elements of the prosecutor's case to the public" a few days before it otherwise would have come out anyway. Without any help from the press, Epstein wrote, the FBI linked the burglars to the White House and traced their money to the Nixon campaign—within a week of the break-in. Woodward and Bernstein "systematically ignored or minimized" the work of law enforcement officials to "focus on those parts" of the story "that were leaked to them," Epstein charged.

Kutler found that "local Washington reporting, especially in the *Post*, closely tracked the FBI's work, relying primarily on raw Bureau reports." [Bob Woodward's] account placing the pair at the center of the scandal, the historian wrote, was "self-serving" and "exaggerated," part of "the press' excessive claims for its role." Indeed, he says, even if media coverage during Watergate had been cautious and passive, Nixon would have been forced out of office because an independent court system combined with a Democratic Congress was intent on getting to the bottom of the scandal.

The fact is, an incredible array of powerful actors all converged on Nixon at once—the FBI, prosecutors, congressional investigators, the judicial system. This included the media. It did not play the leading role, but it did play a role.

"That's 'if' history, and dubious 'if' history at that," Bernstein counters. "You can't write 'if' history; history is what happened. What happened is that the press coverage played a very big role in making information available that the Watergate break-in was part of something vast and criminal and directed from or near the Oval Office against President Nixon's opponents." Bernstein acknowledges that the "role of Bob [Woodward] and myself has been mythologized" because "in great events people look for villains and heroes" and oversimplify what happened. "At the same time, we were in the right place at the right time and did the right thing."

But other academic experts also minimize journalism's impact. In an analysis of polling data measuring so-called "media effects" on public opinion, communication scholars Gladys and Kurt Lang wrote that "the press was a prime mover in the controversy only in its early phase," when the *Post* linked the Watergate burglars to Nixon operatives. Journalism's main contributions to influencing public opinion, the husband-and-wife team found, were covering the unfolding events of the scandal and televising the Senate's Watergate hearings. "That so many of the struggles between Nixon and his opponents played out on television accounts for the impression that the news media and an aroused public opinion forced the downfall of Richard Nixon," the scholars wrote. Journalism may have helped prepare the public ahead of time for Nixon's removal, the authors argued, but it was Congress, not the media, that forced the president's resignation.

Media Coverage of Watergate Forced Authorities to Investigate

Such public opinion polling, however, can be a clumsy way of gauging journalism's impact. The effect of news coverage can be subtle and hard to measure, in part because government investigators may be reluctant to acknowledge that they were responding to publicity; to admit being influenced by journalism could suggest that they weren't properly doing their jobs beforehand. Nonetheless, publicity can push authorities to take action if only to avoid being embarrassed by media disclosures.

"In Watergate," writes historian David Greenberg, author of the new book "Nixon's Shadow," "it was unclear at first whether the FBI would pursue crimes beyond the break-in itself. If the *Post* hadn't kept Watergate alive, it's not certain that the bureau, or the Senate, would have kept digging. Woodward and Bernstein's work shaped the way Watergate unfolded."

According to Woodward, the late Sam Ervin, chairman of the Senate Watergate Committee, "called me and asked questions, and his work grew out of the stories that we did." Woodward also says that after Nixon's resignation, the presiding federal judge, the late John Sirica, told him "flat out" that the *Post*'s stories influenced him to crack down on the Watergate conspirators. "Judges don't decide to get tough in a vacuum," Woodward says. "Senators don't decide to investigate in a vacuum." Both were influenced by the press, Woodward says, because "the process wasn't uncovering the abuses. It's that simple."

Other journalists who covered Watergate agree. "The record clearly shows that the cover-up would have worked if the press hadn't done its job," says CBS News anchorman

Dan Rather, whose aggressive Watergate reporting led the Nixon White House to try to get him fired. Rather maintains that Congress and the courts "didn't have a clue, frankly" about Watergate crimes and that federal investigators wised up "only after repeated and constant coverage" by journalists.

Besides, the battle was political as well as legal, says Jack Nelson, who covered Watergate for the *Los Angeles Times*: "Nixon was fighting not just prosecutors and Congress but also in the court of public opinion. For all of their controlling Congress, the Democrats were not in any sense going to go after Nixon unless the public was behind it. And the public got behind it because of the press holding Nixon's feet to the fire."

But Watergate prosecutor Seymour Glanzer says that what really mattered—both legally and politically—was Nixon's failure to destroy his incriminating tape recordings, not the media's coverage: "Woodward and Bernstein followed in our wake. The idea that they were this great investigative team was a bunch of baloney." Glanzer believes that an official in the FBI's Washington field office leaked details of the Watergate probe to other reporters besides Woodward and Bernstein but that only the *Post* published them early on because of its larger ongoing "struggle with the White House."

Several Newspapers Besides the *Post* Contributed to the Coverage

There is no dispute that the *Post* led other media in the early coverage of Watergate. According to a quantitative analysis by University of Illinois professor Louis W. Liebovich, in the critical first six months after the break-in, the *Post* published some 200 news articles about Watergate, more than double the number of its nearest competitor, the *New York Times*. "Many of the *Washington Post* stories were carried on page one," Liebovich found, play that occurred "only occasionally" in other newspapers after the initial publicity about the break-in died down. In addition, *Post* stories were more often investigative in nature and "revealed new details about covert activities directed by the White House," while other news organizations "rarely carried their own enterprise stories."

However, the *Post*'s lead diminished later in the scandal

as other journalists also uncovered wrongdoing by Nixon
and his men. The late Clark Mollenhoff, an investigative reporter who not only covered Watergate for the *Des Moines
Register* but also at one point worked for Nixon, compiled a
list of more than three dozen journalists besides Woodward
and Bernstein who, he said, "made equally great contributions to the success of the Watergate probe." That undoubtedly overstates the case. But, says University of Virginia political scientist Larry Sabato, other reporters "got too little
credit and the *Washington Post* got too much." According to
Nixon White House counsel John W. Dean, as the scandal
developed, the reporter "who does the most devastating
pieces that strike awfully close to home was Sy Hersh" whom
the *New York Times* assigned to the story.

The *Los Angeles Times* also dug up scoops "of the same
caliber of Woodward and Bernstein," says investigative reporter James Polk, then with the *Washington Star*, "but the
L.A. Times wasn't read in Washington" as widely as the *Post*
and therefore didn't have the same degree of influence.
Harvard's Kalb, who was then a correspondent in Washington for CBS News, credits *Post* Executive Editor Ben
Bradlee's "gutsy front-page placement" of Watergate stories
as "crucial because there is no paper in Washington like the
Post. It is the heart and soul of journalism here. . . . Everyone would pick up the *Post* every morning and read the latest bombshell about Watergate."

The *Post* also faced down both public attacks and private intimidation from the Nixon administration. John
Mitchell, Nixon's attorney general, warned Bernstein that
his boss, Publisher Katharine Graham, was "gonna get her
tit caught in a big fat wringer" as a result of his Watergate
reporting. And Nixon himself privately threatened "damnable, damnable problems" for the *Post* when it came to getting its television station licenses renewed.

But here, too, the *Post* was not alone. The Nixon administration variously investigated, wiretapped and audited the
income tax returns of numerous reporters. In all, more than
50 journalists appeared on a special White House "enemies
list." Nixon's otherwise pro-business Justice Department
filed antitrust charges against all three broadcast networks.
As Woodward reported a year after Nixon's resignation,
Nixon himself allegedly ordered an aide to falsely smear
syndicated columnist Jack Anderson as a homosexual, and

two White House aides held a clandestine meeting to plot ways to poison the troublesome journalist. In many respects, reporters who investigated Nixon were less hunters than prey.

As a whole, most Washington journalists during Watergate were neither victims nor heroes; few challenged the Nixon White House's version of events during the pivotal first months of the scandal. "Too many people in the press bought into the assumption that there was a 'New Nixon,'" Bernstein remembers, and that Watergate "could not have involved the White House." Historian Kutler dissected the "almost nonexistent" media coverage that took place long after the break-in, when for months "fewer than 15 of the more than 430 reporters in Washington worked exclusively on Watergate."

Only after Congress and the courts started to expose evidence of White House criminality did the rest of the media finally jump on the story. But coverage then became a feeding frenzy of often inaccurate reporting. CBS anchorman Walter Cronkite falsely implicated White House aide Patrick Buchanan in money-laundering. The *New York Times'* Jeff Gerth, then a freelance writer, claimed that Nixon's supposed financial ties to Mafia financier Meyer Lansky and Teamsters boss Jimmy Hoffa meant that "organized crime put its own man in the White House." "In learning from Watergate," wrote Rutgers University professor David Greenberg, reporters "too often emulated not the trailblazers whose skepticism had produced fruitful inquiries but the latecomers who jumped on Watergate only as it was becoming a media spectacle."

"Look," says historian Kutler, "everybody did Watergate and everybody wants credit for it. The fact is, an incredible array of powerful actors all converged on Nixon at once—the FBI, prosecutors, congressional investigators, the judicial system. This included the media. It did not play the leading role, but it did play a role."

The *Post* Kept the Watergate Issue Alive

Ultimately, this role was more complex than many realize, says former Nixon aide Dean: "People think that the *Post* cracked the case and they really didn't. Not to take anything away from the *Post*; it was the only paper that really did any coverage of Watergate early on." But the newspaper's real value, Dean argues, was that it did "just enough to keep the story alive" by lending "legitimacy to those [in the government] who were investigating the scandal." Later in the saga, Dean says, "there is no question that the Senate Watergate hearings and prosecutors were feeding off the media attention they were getting" and "wouldn't have gone as long or as deep but for the frenzy" of press coverage.

In the end, the differing interpretations of Watergate may say as much about those who hold them as they do about what really happened 30 years ago. After all, reporters cover stories close up, focusing on details as events are still unfolding, when ultimate outcomes are unpredictable and unknowable. Historians and sociologists, on the other hand, view the news from afar, when events in retrospect can seem preordained and inevitable.

3

Media Coverage of Watergate Was Not Responsible Journalism

Norman Solomon

Since Richard Nixon's resignation in 1974, the field of investigative journalism has attracted modest numbers of youthful news reporters seeking to break an important story to the public. Though the public imagination was captured by the image of the investigative journalist as a good-guy, truth seeker, the reality of Watergate journalism was a much different story. Author and columnist Norman Solomon argues that out of the two thousand journalists working in Washington during the scandal, only six were working on the Watergate case on a full-time basis. He also contends that the journalists who were closest to the president, the White House press corps, did not ask the tough questions during press conferences that might have forced the president's exposure. The era's press corps was, in the tradition of white-gloves treatment of the office of the president, not the adversarial press of the modern day.

F or a long time after the arrests of five burglars at the Democratic National Committee's executive offices in the early morning of June 17, 1972, the conventional media wisdom was to accept the White House depiction of a minor crime without any political significance. During that summer and fall, few journalists devoted much time to probing the Watergate incident as President Nixon cruised to a landslide re-election victory in November.

Norman Solomon, "Three Decades Later, Watergate Is a Cautionary Tale," www. alternet.org, June 13, 2002. Copyright © 2002 by Alternet. Reproduced by permission.

Few Reporters Actually Covered Watergate

"At the time of Watergate, there were some 2,000 full-time reporters in Washington, working for major news organizations," [*Washington Post* reporter Carl] Bernstein later pointed out. "In the first six months after the break-in . . . 14 of those reporters were assigned by their news organizations to cover the Watergate story on a full-time basis, and of these 14, half-a-dozen on what you might call an investigative basis."

Speaking at Harvard's Institute of Politics in 1989, Bernstein added: "The press has been engaged in a kind of orgy of self-congratulations about our performance in Watergate and about our performance in covering the news since. And it seems to me no attitude could be more unjustified." He was right on target.

Investigating a President Was Not Standard Procedure

Helen Thomas is one of the most seasoned and candid members of the White House press corps. "We realize that we did a lousy job on Watergate," she has recalled. "We just sat there and took what they said at face value."

That's been pretty standard media practice. Presidential assertions get the benefit of many doubts. And before the press declares a major national scandal, some movers and shakers need to be riled up.

A central factor in the Watergate story was that it involved foul play by one elite faction against another. The bungled burglary at the Watergate complex 30 years ago was part of a furtive illicit operation by a Republican organization, the Committee to Re-Elect the President (with the apt acronym CREEP), to filch documents from the headquarters of the other corporate party.

But what if—instead of being implicated in a burglary at a Democratic Party office—the White House had been implicated in a break-in aimed at a political party without power? We don't have to speculate. Throughout the Watergate era, the U.S. government was committing far worse political crimes against the Socialist Workers Party. Meanwhile, no journalists with mainstream clout ever seemed to care.

A retrospective *Los Angeles Times* article, published in 1995, summarized the historical record: "For 38 years, the

FBI waged a campaign of infiltration and harassment against a small Trotskyite organization called the Socialist Workers Party. The bureau staged burglaries, planted fake news stories and otherwise sought to discredit the party and its members, who, though pushing a radical political agenda, were engaging in peaceful and lawful political behavior. The 38 years, which ended in 1976, produced not a single arrest."

Watergate Reporting Should Not Be a Model Standard

Instead of viewing the best Watergate reporting as a model to build on, for the most part the biggest media outlets soon regarded it as a laurel to rest on. Before his retirement, *Washington Post* executive editor Ben Bradlee acknowledged as much in an interview with author Mark Hertsgaard about a dozen years after President Nixon's forced resignation. "The criticism was that we were going on too much, and trying to make a Watergate out of everything," Bradlee said. "And I think we were sensitive to that criticism much more than we should have been, and that we did ease off."

While fond of posturing as intrepid watchdogs, the major news media are still inclined to ease off. The overall dynamic could be described as "aggressive-passive." The watchdogs growl sometimes, while routinely wagging their tails.

Chapter 3

The Legacy
of Watergate

1

Watergate Led to Major Government Reform

William L. Chaze

In the years following Watergate, Congress placed restrictions on the kinds of information that are legitimately protected under executive privilege. Congress also tried to counter American cynicism and distrust of government by passing the Freedom of Information Act, allowing citizens unprecedented access to previously unreleased documents, and a number of other "good government" reforms. These included new codes of congressional conduct that revoked franking privileges, office slush funds, and required annual filing of personal financial statements and a 1974 campaign reform law limiting contributions to federal candidates and requiring detailed expenditure reports.

When Republican Ronald Reagan was sworn in as president in 1980, he faced a powerful Democratic majority in Congress that had weakened the office of the president by passing several reforms that made the president more accountable for his actions. In the following *U.S. News & World Report* article, journalist William L. Chaze maintains that the office of the president has shifted from an imperial office, left fairly unchecked by Congress, to an office that is surrounded by restrictive reform measures. Chaze contends that by holding government officials to stricter standards, by scrutinizing presidential decisions, by lifting the cloak of executive privilege, and by granting investigative bodies more independence, the conditions that encouraged the Watergate scandal will be less likely to reoccur in the future.

Ten years ago on August 9, a disgraced Richard Nixon ended a national nightmare by resigning the Presidency under threat of impeachment.

Today, the lasting significance of the events [that] began with a botched burglary of the Democratic headquarters in Washington's Watergate office complex and ended with the fall of an administration is still hotly debated.

Evidence of Watergate's impact abounds—a less arrogant Presidency, a more assertive Congress, a more responsible Federal Bureau of Investigation and Central Intelligence Agency, a more open bureaucracy and a more tightly controlled federal-election system.

The scandal's chief legacy, in the view of many experts, has been to instill in all public officials a sense of accountability often missing before Watergate. "In all three branches of government," observes senior FBI aide John Hotis, "officials now look not only at the legality of their conduct but also the propriety."

Ethical standards, say officials, are much higher than in Nixon's day. "People are much more aware and sophisticated about the potential for appearances of impropriety."

But with the dimming of memories—dramatized by Nixon's own emergence from the shadows of disgrace—many experts see the changes wrought by Watergate becoming blurred as the government slides back to its pre-Watergate ways. "For a time, Washington seemed aware of the dangerous fruits of secrecy," says Archibald Cox, the special Watergate prosecutor fired by Nixon. "Unfortunately, there is reason to believe the lesson is being forgotten."

Of most concern to reformers like Cox: The continuing impact of big-money contributors on politics, a Reagan administration drive to weaken post-Watergate restrictions on the FBI and revelations that the CIA still conducts covert activities without fully informing responsible officials.

The Watergate crucible showed that the system of checks and balances worked, but it exposed serious problems—a Presidency that had become all-powerful, a growing government taste for secrecy, a political system rife with corruption and a Congress reluctant to probe the Executive Branch.

The reform mood that swept the capital in the scandal's aftermath spawned many changes. Politicians were subjected to new ethics and campaign rules. The intelligence community came under close scrutiny. Federal agencies moved to insulate themselves against further abuses. Procedures were established under the Freedom of Information Act for public access to previously withheld government records. And Congress, anxious to end the "imperial Presidency," sought to regain its lost status as a coequal branch.

The Public Harbors Cynicism Toward the President

Watergate's shadow lies most heavily over the White House.

Aides must now comply with both tough ethics standards and rules that discourage use of federal agencies for political purposes—a major contributor to Nixon's downfall.

Most important, experts conclude, is that the public no longer perceives the President as a near-mythical being who can do no wrong. The trust-shattering combination of Watergate and Vietnam, followed by the weakened tenures of Presidents [Gerald] Ford and [Jimmy] Carter, ended that. Explains Thomas Cronin, professor of political science at Colorado College: "The storybook or the textbook Presidency—the romanticized view taught to schoolchildren that the President must know best—is no longer present."

Adds political scientist Louis W. Koenig of New York University: "The Presidency has come off its pedestal."

The Presidency today is a far cry from the office as Nixon and some of his predecessors knew it. Apart from Vietnam, Nixon conducted foreign policy with little interference from Congress. When he found fault with budget outlays, he impounded funds. When oversight of federal agencies became a problem, he appointed department heads as White House counselors, thus shielding them from a prying Congress under a cloak of "executive privilege."

Ronald Reagan's powers are more limited. Although hailed as the strongest post-Watergate President, he often complains of undue constraints placed on him by Congress, particularly in the areas of budget and foreign affairs. Also the Supreme Court has barred Presidents from holding back appropriated funds and from imposing so-called executive privilege to shield illegalities.

Current Officials Held to Stricter Standards

Where Nixon and his predecessors often exposed U.S. troops to hostile situations abroad, Reagan must seek Congress's approval. Last winter [December 1982], the lawmakers invoked the War Powers Act—a byproduct of Vietnam and Watergate—to impose an 18-month deadline on U.S. participation in the multinational peacekeeping force in Lebanon. More recently, they shut off U.S. aid to the CIA-backed rebels fighting Nicaragua's leftist government.

The changes go beyond power. Ethical standards, say officials, are much higher than in Nixon's day. "People are much more aware and sophisticated about the potential for appearances of impropriety," comments White House legal counsel Fred Fielding, who brings to his present job the perspective of a man who also served Nixon as an aide.

Stricter standards are evident in the fate of several Reagan administration officials, starting with former national security adviser Richard Allen. Allen felt obliged to quit in 1982 amid a dispute over the origin and purpose of $1,000 in cash that turned up in his office safe.

Similarly, Max Hugel had only briefly been chief of the CIA's clandestine operations when he was asked to step down because of questions about his business dealings. A dozen top officials of the Environmental Protection Agency quit in a flap over political misuse of the Superfund toxic-waste cleanup program. Currently, the Justice Department has an independent investigator looking into the finances of Edwin Meese, Reagan's nominee for Attorney General.

Closer scrutiny by Congress, law-enforcement agencies and the press has prompted the White House to be more cautious about its nominees for key positions. For one thing, when running background checks on presidential appointees, the FBI now asks if candidates ever have been targets of lawsuits, investigations or censure by professional groups.

Only three weeks after the current administration came to power, Fielding set rules requiring White House aides to go through his office whenever they had questions for the Justice Department on specific investigations. "The rules have been very effective," he says. "There have been a couple of instances where people have gone out of track. I can think of four or five cases in four years. That's not bad."

Experts disagree as to whether, on balance, Watergate

changed the White House for the better. One school argues that an imperial Presidency has been so emasculated by post-Watergate laws that it has become the imperiled Presidency, unable to act decisively.

Another holds that a skillful President still can lead effectively. "You get a Roosevelt or a Reagan in there and things turn around real fast," contends Professor Koenig. "It's obvious from Reagan's performance that a lot depends on who's there."

Watergate Forced Congress to Scrutinize Future Presidents

On Capitol Hill, Watergate accelerated a process that had begun earlier with discontent over the Vietnam War.

Unilateral actions of Presidents during the war—among them the secret bombing of Cambodia ordered by Nixon—led lawmakers to [begin] challenging the Chief Executive's role in foreign policy. One important step: The War Powers Act of 1973, limiting a President's authority to involve the U.S. in hostilities abroad.

Vietnam planted seeds of distrust in a Congress that more often than not had been deferential in its approach to the Presidency. Lawmakers had tended to ask few questions, even renewing a Nixon "discretionary" fund after being told its purpose was none of their business.

Congress was accustomed to exercising only sporadic oversight of federal agencies. Although Senate and House committees ultimately helped expose the facts of Watergate, the initial reaction was a characteristic indifference.

Coming on top of Vietnam, Watergate was the last straw. It left Congress combative, more partisan and ready to buck the White House at virtually every turn.

Determined to reassert themselves on budgetary matters as well as foreign policy, post-Watergate lawmakers created a Congressional Budget Office to produce a spending plan to compete with the President's. A desire for independent data of all kinds helped swell the congressional staff from 14,539 in 1973 to more than 20,000 at present—at a cost topping 642 million dollars a year.

Today, hundreds of staffers are assigned to monitor government agencies, including the CIA and other intelligence-gathering bodies. Between them, the House and Senate have nearly 60 employes riding herd over espionage agencies at a cost of more than 2.5 million dollars a year.

But the agencies being watched do not always cooperate. A recent case in point: The CIA's secret mining of Nicaraguan harbors, an activity that seemed to breach agreements requiring that Congress be informed of such covert operations. "It's the same old story," commented a senior aide to the House Select Committee on Intelligence. "If you don't know the right question to ask, you don't get the information."

Another congressional response to Watergate was enactment of ethics measures affecting all of government.

Watchdog inspectors general were assigned to federal departments to root out wrongdoing. An Office of Government Ethics was created to police conflict-of-interest and disclosure rules. A mechanism—so far seldom used—was provided for the Justice Department to seek appointment of a special prosecutor to probe official misconduct. And, in an attempt to prevent political misuse of the Internal Revenue Service, strict limits were placed on disclosure of tax-return information.

Coming on top of Vietnam, Watergate was the last straw. It left Congress combative, more partisan and ready to buck the White House at virtually every turn.

Congress also set about reforming itself. Financial-disclosure laws were adopted. A revolt against powerful committee chairmen was led by the "Watergate class" of 1974—members elected at the height of indignation over the scandal. The importance of seniority was downgraded, and more of the business of Congress was opened to the public.

Despite such efforts, Congress was stunned by a series of revelations of corruption among its own members. Post-Watergate years saw more lawmakers than administration officials cited and punished for various offenses. In the Abscam scandal[1] alone, seven members of Congress were convicted of bribe taking or related charges.

Now, say many lawmakers, much of the power Congress

---

1. Abscam refers to the FBI operation where agents, posing as Arabs, offered select public officials bribes in return for political favors.

accumulated after Watergate appears to be shifting back to the White House. "The President was weaker for a time," observes Representative Don Edwards (D-Calif.). "But under Reagan, a very aggressive President who goes his own way, the President's power is increasing in issues involving foreign policy, civil rights and education, among others."

FBI Gains More Independence After Watergate

In Nixon's era, questionable White House demands on the Justice Department and FBI were routine.

At one point, the FBI was asked to devote itself to the task of providing data on criminal-justice issues that might help Nixon in his 1972 campaign. As Watergate unfolded, the White House even requested—and obtained—confidential summaries of FBI interviews with Nixon aides.

That would not happen today, say knowledgeable sources. Now, the FBI chief serves a 10-year nonrenewable term, which helps shield him from political pressure. Formal guidelines have been established for FBI dealings with the White House and the Attorney General. Rules limit the scope of criminal investigations, intelligence gathering and background checks of prospective federal appointees.

Many law-enforcement abuses that came to light in the early 1970s involved overzealous efforts to investigate so-called subversives, many of whom were guilty only of criticizing Nixon. Phones of government officials, reporters and political activists were tapped and anti-Nixon groups infiltrated by undercover agents.

Such activities have been reduced substantially by laws making it harder to obtain permission for wiretaps on national-security grounds, and by the FBI's own guidelines limiting investigations of suspected subversives. Nowadays, the bureau is involved in only a few dozen security investigations at any time, in contrast to thousands of cases under way in the last years of [former FBI director] J. Edgar Hoover.

"From all we know, the FBI is focusing on criminal cases, not on lawful political activity," says Jerry Berman of the American Civil Liberties Union, which monitors FBI activities. "This is a major change—a bench mark—that Watergate helped to produce. There is no evidence that the FBI is playing political games with the White House."

As a direct result of Watergate, a major overhaul of

campaign-finance laws was undertaken in 1974.

Amid high-minded talk of cleansing the political system, the Federal Election Commission was set up to enforce disclosure of campaign expenditures, and federal financing of presidential elections was enacted. Among other things, the goal was to discourage illegal corporate contributions such as those funneled into Nixon's 1972 re-election drive.

A decade later, critics say the reforms have proved sorely inadequate as specialists have found ways to render meaningless the limits on both spending and contributions. Moreover, the commission rarely examines campaign reports submitted by members of Congress.

Myriad loopholes have allowed candidates and parties to evade the law's purpose. For instance, nothing prohibits parties from regularly collecting and shipping contributions to states with few or no spending limits. There it is used to help federal as well as state and local candidates—all legal as long as the money is spent by the state organizations for party-building activity.

Both major parties are using large sums of corporate money to pay for party-headquarters expenses, with no disclosure required. Those contributions, in turn, free millions in party funds for campaigning. The law limits only those corporate contributions that go directly to candidates.

Nor do spending limits apply to so-called independent outlays that a group makes on behalf of a candidate without specific authorization. Political action committees—PAC's —set up by corporations, trade groups and others are permitted to spend as much as they wish as long as they do not operate in concert with the candidate's campaign.

"Everyone wanted to be as clean as Caesar's wife when the Watergate hearings were on," noted a legal expert in campaign finance. "Now, the attitude has changed tremendously. People aren't threatened with the prospect of going to jail, so they pretty much do as they please."

2

The White House–Press Relationship Has Been Adversarial Since Watergate

Louis W. Liebovich

Until the Nixon presidency, U.S. presidents enjoyed generally positive relationships with the members of the press. From the outset, however, the Nixon administration planned strategies to thwart journalists' attempts to collect and disseminate information. Nixon maintained a tight control over his foreign and domestic policies, and his press secretary Ronald Ziegler was perceived by the press corps as less than open on important issues. In thwarting and antagonizing the press, Nixon drew negative press accounts that affected his public approval ratings, something he sorely resented throughout his political career and blamed when Watergate bloomed into a national crisis. The press pursuit gave rise to the term "attack journalism," in which the line between truly newsworthy bad acts and everyday human frailties is often blurred. In the years since Nixon's presidency, the relationship between the press and the president has continued to decline. In the following selection, journalist Louis W. Liebovich explains how each president since Nixon has failed to reestablish a positive media relationship. He contends that the duties of the White House press secretary have shifted from disseminating information to managing the president's public image, controlling the flow of criticism rather than sharing information. He also contends that an adversarial press now actively seeks to discredit public officials, intensifying public cynicism toward the president and other public officials.

B eginning with [President] Theodore Roosevelt and ending with [President John F.] Kennedy, the presidency had been strengthened almost continuously for sixty-two years, as had the role of the press in affecting national public policy and the presidency. Not all chief executives during this period were celebrated. Warren Harding, a newspaper publisher by trade, was one of the least effective presidents of all time. His heirs, Calvin Coolidge and Herbert Hoover, similarly are rated among the nation's least effective chief executives, and not all presidents, even those rated by historians as notable, were popular with the press, either. But the most renowned ones recognized that good or, at the very least, tolerable relations with news media were necessary to promote programs and influence the Congress and the public. Theodore Roosevelt, Woodrow Wilson, Franklin Roosevelt, Harry Truman, Dwight Eisenhower, and John [F.] Kennedy have all been ranked among the most successful presidents in history, and each either was able to charm reporters or had press officers who served as effective intermediaries. But if 1962 was the zenith of the presidency, the euphoria quickly eroded after the assassination, ending the public's love affair. Lyndon Johnson succeeded Kennedy and is highly rated by historians. Yet, he failed to establish positive press relations and was driven from office by a negative image and an unpopular war that was depicted graphically on television news nightly, illustrating that legislative achievement in modern times is not always accompanied by public acclaim. Richard Nixon and Watergate followed, and, by the mid-1970s, contentious give-and-take press relations had been replaced by pure antagonism. As we enter the twenty-first century, the situation has not improved, but instead has deteriorated. Public policy, public awareness of issues and events, and the popularity of both press and president have suffered.

Press Relations First Deteriorate in the 1960s

How did this occur? How is it that between 1962 and 1974 we evolved from presidential worship to widespread scorn?

Vietnam and Watergate are only parts of the answer. The downswing is a complex mosaic of changed technology, altered social mores, a reinvented White House press office, adjusted perceptions by reporters and editors, altered press strategies, and public skepticism followed by popular indifference.

The press and public had become cynical and suspicious. Nixon responded in kind. From the day he took office, he declared war on reporters.

Problems in the White House began almost immediately after Kennedy's death. Johnson alternately tried to bully and coddle reporters with little success. The War in Southeast Asia and the fabricated statements and figures issued continuously by the White House were only part of the failure with the press of his administration. As the last in a string of presidents who had popularized the presidency, Kennedy took fame to a different level. As the missile crisis indicates, Kennedy (also his wife, Jacqueline, at times) was more adept at popularizing and personalizing than he was at establishing effective policy. For instance, the handling of the missile crisis, in retrospect, suggests that Kennedy's perceived weakness in the Soviet Union touched off the crisis initially. Then a confrontation and finally an agreement by the United States never to invade Cuba brought on a most serious crisis with the most dangerous of potential consequences, followed by a concession that has left Castro in power for more than four decades. Yet, Kennedy was lauded at the time on all sides. The presidency was not only at its popular height by 1962, but also had been transformed into a Hollywood-style personalization, where style not only won over substance, but obliterated it. This trend accelerated in the 1970s as Americans immersed themselves in the private lives of famous people. *People* magazine epitomized the celebrity journalism that previously had been quarantined to the entertainment and gossip pages.

Concurrently while he was president, Kennedy flip-flopped the roles of print and broadcast media among the Washington hierarchy. Television became the preeminent medium, replacing newspapers and news magazines, because Kennedy placed his primary emphasis on providing news to television reporters and anchors. These two developments hindered subsequent presidents, especially Lyndon Johnson, whose forte was not suave rejoinders at press conferences or gregarious discussions with pesky journalists, but backroom wheeling and dealing. His image fit neither television nor a personalized presidency, and that misfortune was handed such heirs as Nixon, Gerald Ford, and George [H.W.] Bush.

Richard Nixon Declares War on Reporters

Richard Nixon's problems in the 1970s were compounded by the outrage that followed revelations about doctored Johnson Administration casualty figures in Vietnam and overly optimistic reports about troop successes in the field, and public disclosures that Kennedy had been a philanderer. The press and public had become cynical and suspicious. Nixon responded in kind. From the day he took office, he declared war on reporters. Unlike any other previous presidency of the century the Nixon administration set out exclusively in 1969 to manipulate reporters and control the information flow from the Oval Office. Even during the Hoover administration, when press relations turned so sour that nearly all communications between reporters and the president ceased by 1932, there had been valiant attempts on both sides to reach an accord in 1929, so that news could flow smoothly from the White House. Though Hoover saw reporters mostly as either friends or antagonists, he was willing to work with them as a group for nearly half of his term in office. Nixon's people made no such effort.

When Nixon took office, he split the White House communications duties between Herbert Klein, director of communications, and Ronald Ziegler, press secretary. Klein was in charge of promoting Nixon's image and ideas, and Ziegler, at age twenty-nine, was responsible for handling reporters. In truth, however, both took orders from Chief-of-Staff H.R. Haldeman, who met daily with Nixon to plot public-relations ploys and ways to frustrate and impede White House correspondents. Both Klein and Ziegler were then given their orders in a flurry of daily Haldeman memos, until Nixon's chief of staff was forced to resign in April 1973 after Watergate had already overwhelmed the presidency. This system resulted in planned public verbal attacks on the press by Vice President Spiro Agnew, a blizzard of daily public relations–oriented press releases, a paucity of presidential press conferences, and finally illegal spying and wiretaps. Watergate was not so much a "third-rate burglary," as Ziegler so ineptly described it in the summer of 1972, as it was the ultimate end to a paranoid, hostile strategy toward correspondents and political opponents.

Press Relations Evolve into Public Relations Tactics

Yet, this adversarial mentality came to be the norm for the next twenty-six years. Gerald Ford's untimely pardon of Nixon in September 1974 and Gerald terHorst's subsequent resignation as [White House] press secretary ensured that no working journalist would again be asked to serve as press secretary after Ford was defeated at the polls. Instead, the office came to be a repository for public relations experts whose concerns for burnishing images far exceeded any interests in legitimate news flow. [Former presidents] Jimmy Carter, Ronald Reagan, and Bill Clinton all worked television to great advantage, until the flow of history and their own personal shortcomings turned against them. To a great extent, Reagan's coterie of advisers employed the tactics first attempted by Nixon's people: manipulating daily news flow, carefully controlling the few press conferences he held, concentrating on a television image, answering few questions from reporters, and boiling policy statements down to a few sound bites. Only George [H.W.] Bush attempted to establish positive and lasting relationships with reporters, and his lack of success at the ballot box in 1992 left an indelible impression on subsequent candidates.

Journalists Report Gossip Instead of Issues

When presidential candidate Gary Hart in 1987 challenged reporters to follow him around if they suspected that he had been unfaithful to his wife, a new era of reporting was born. Gossipy, tawdry journalism already employed in other news stories soon infected White House coverage. Too many reporters spent inordinate portions of their time pursuing rumors and gossip about personal indiscretions. At the same time, networks, news magazines, and newspapers tightened their fiscal belts in the 1980s, bringing less-experienced reporters to Washington and spending less on costly, detailed stories at a time when information outlets were vastly expanding. By the time Bill Clinton ran for president in 1992, reporting on personal minutiae too often supplanted issue-oriented stories, and gossip replaced fact-finding. Reporters commonly clamored for the most trivial detail from a candidate's personal past, while leaving voters uninformed on pressing issues of the day.

The president was no longer portrayed in popular media as a courageous and admirable leader, but as a grimy, scheming politician with the morals of a drunken sailor.

Each pebble tossed into the presidential pond had rippled for three decades, finally reaching shore in the 1990s. Public evaluation of the press deteriorated rapidly, and the president was no longer portrayed in popular media as a courageous and admirable leader, but as a grimy, scheming politician with the morals of a drunken sailor. Elections had become fund-raising marathons with media declaring front-runners two years before the election. Primaries proliferated. Some mutated into undemocratic straw polls and caucuses, which reflected only the necessity to capture media attention in a desperate struggle to raise more money to spend on—you guessed it media.

By 1996, the presidential election process had alienated voters. Interest in the election plummeted to an all-time low with voter participation hovering at the 50-percent level and the election campaign relegated to the back pages of newspapers and the fourth story in evening broadcasts. Clinton's second term, during the greatest economic boom in history, came to be dominated by a sex scandal involving a twenty-four-year-old White House intern and an impeachment process, the epitome of capital politics and Washington journalism gone awry. Not a single president after Lyndon Johnson has been rated highly by historians, and the presidential-election process seems at the dawn of the twenty-first century to be bogged down because of a gossipy press and unfair financial restrictions.

Will a new millennium bring more of the same? Trends in journalism develop over many years, and initial coverage of the 2000 election suggests that no upward trend has yet evolved. However, many news organizations have begun to reexamine their news policies with regard to presidential politics and elections. Some have consciously chosen to downplay unseemly and unsubstantiated stories that might have been trumpeted in the past. Others have tried to act more responsibly in covering issues and offering opportunities for candidates to air their views on important, relevant topics. Networks have recognized the need to avoid sound-bite journalism. Some networks, news magazines, and newspapers have offered free time or space to presidential candidates to discuss campaign issues. These tactics have not always worked, but there has been a recognition of a need to try something new.

What will likely change the trend is a strong president who rises above the restrictive coverage of the day and who works well with reporters. This person will have to be free of nearly all past indiscretions, be able to raise tens of millions of dollars for campaigns, be photogenic on television, be persuasive enough to work with a recalcitrant Congress, and be able to campaign nearly non-stop for months and years at a time. Journalism and the presidency have both run in cycles, and some of our greatest leaders have risen when the presidency was dominated by mediocrity (Lincoln, for example). We ask a lot of our president as a new century dawns because both press and president have stockpiled a multitude of sins from the past and the relationship—an important link—has come to be dominated by mutual antagonism. As it always has, however, that nexus is bound to change; that is the thought which provides optimism for the coming generation.

3

Watergate Eroded Public Trust in Government

Bill Schneider

Americans' confidence that their government could be trusted to do the right thing began to waver in the mid-1960s, as the war in Vietnam escalated, campus protests grew, and race riots erupted in major cities. Public trust collapsed completely with Watergate, as criminal conspiracies were revealed at the highest levels of government and a presidency was disgraced and finally dismantled. Since 1974 nothing has happened to restore public trust: Most people continue to believe government is incapable of solving problems, and enduring public contempt for professional politicians is a major factor in the political rise of outsiders and nonprofessionals such as businessman Ross Perot and General Colin Powell.

Political commentator Bill Schneider is the senior political analyst for CNN, which he joined in 1991. Schneider is a resident fellow at the American Enterprise Institute, a leading conservative think tank in Washington, D.C., and a contributing editor on politics and public opinion to the *Atlantic Monthly*, the *Los Angeles Times*, and the *New Republic*.

What's been the most powerful force in American politics [since 1974]? In a word, it's cynicism. Americans have come to believe the worst about government, politics and politicians. It didn't start with Watergate, but Watergate turned an erosion of public confidence into a collapse.

Remember when government worked and Americans trusted their leaders? No? Then you must be too young to remember the Eisenhower and Kennedy eras. The federal government had rescued the country from the Great Depression. It had won a world war. And it was using its power to bring about social justice in America.

Kennedy was the last president of that golden era. "The energy, the faith, the devotion which we bring to this endeavor will light our country and all who serve it, and the glow from that fire will truly light the world," Kennedy declared.

Watergate also heightened public contempt for professional politicians and created a market for outsiders and nonprofessionals.

Polls taken in 1958 and 1964 showed three-quarters of Americans believed they could trust the government in Washington to do what was right. Three quarters. Imagine!

In 1965, everything began to fall apart. There was the escalation of the Vietnam War, a wave of campus protests, and a race riot in Los Angeles. Government could not cope. Public trust began to erode.

The percentage of Americans who said they trusted the government in Washington fell to 65 percent in 1966, 61 percent in 1968, and 53 percent in 1970.

Watergate Was the Last Straw

The downturn came to a climax with Watergate. Americans saw a presidency disintegrate before their eyes, criminal conspiracies at the highest level of government and a president driven out of office. The effect on public trust was immediate and dramatic.

Watergate crushed the public's faith in government. In 1974, a little more than a third of Americans—36 percent—said they still trusted the government. Since Watergate, nothing has happened to restore public trust. In the 1970s, the economy began a long period of deterioration. We suffered military humiliation, first in Vietnam, then in Iran.

Not only did government fail to solve those problems, but people believed government caused problems like inflation. Ironically, the collapse of confidence in government gave Republicans a big opportunity. After all, they're the party that claims government doesn't work.

By 1980, Americans believed it, and elected Ronald Reagan.

The Reagan economic boom had the unintended consequence of boosting trust in government, which rose to 44 percent in 1984, but nowhere near where it used to be. And only until the next recession. [In 1997, twenty-five years after Watergate], times are pretty good. The economy is booming. Crime is down. The U.S. is the world's only superpower. What's happening to public trust?

It's up—to 32 percent. That's nowhere near where the country was before Watergate. In fact, it's just about where the country was after Watergate. As the saying goes, "Been down so long, it looks like up to me."

Contempt for Politicians Endures

Watergate also heightened public contempt for professional politicians and created a market for outsiders and nonprofessionals, like Jimmy Carter, Reagan, Ross Perot and Colin Powell.

People expect them to rescue the country from all that cynicism.

4

Watergate's Lasting Lessons in the Use and Abuse of Language

Hugh Rank

An important legacy of Watergate was in raising public awareness of the political manipulation of language; of the need for
critical analysis of language to expose political doublespeak,
propaganda, and illegal activity; and to infer the true character
of elected officials. The public learned this lesson in two
stages. First, in televised congressional hearings in 1973, witness after witness delivered a barrage of inflated, legalistic jargon; stock phrases and circumlocution; and euphemisms intended to downplay the scandal. Instead, however, the
testimony provoked ridicule, doubt, and further examination:
This kind of speech simply was not believable. Then in 1974,
transcripts of taped Oval Office conversations exposed President Richard Nixon as a liar and a vulgar, suspicious, and vin-
dictive man, his speech shockingly at odds with his self-
righteous public persona. This speech was all too believable,
and led directly to Nixon's resignation. Since Watergate, the
disillusioned public has been wisely reluctant to take political
or corporate rhetoric at face value. Training in recognizing
propaganda techniques was incorporated in high school and
college-level language curricula, and a host of "truth-in-" laws
were established to force full disclosure, in plain language, in
lending, packaging, advertising, and campaign finance.

Hugh Rank is professor emeritus at Governors State University in University Park, Illinois, where he taught English
from 1972 to 1999. During the Watergate era, Rank chaired the
Committee on Public Doublespeak of the National Council of

Hugh Rank, "Watergate and the Language," *Language and Public Policy*, edited by
Hugh Rank. Urbana, IL: National Council of Teachers of English, 1974. Copyright
© 1974 by the National Council of Teachers of English. Reproduced by permission.

Teachers of English (NCTE). He is the developer of Intensify/ Downplay, a teaching tool for the analysis of propaganda techniques in advertising, the media, and political rhetoric.

The political phenomenon of Watergate will affect the study of history, politics, and government, at all levels from the elementary school classes in "Civics" and "Current Events" to the curricula of the graduate schools and law schools. But it is also likely that the impact of Watergate will be found in the teaching of language arts. For millions of Americans who witnessed, Watergate was a war of words, a drama of language manipulation.

After two years of investigation and controversy, two events especially focused public attention on the use and abuse of language: the televised congressional hearings in the summer of 1973, and the release of the White House transcripts in the late spring of 1974. During the televised hearings, the various linguistic issues ranged from random charges of "grammatical errors" to formal charges of legal perjury. Some people were concerned that Standard English Usage was being violated, while others responded to the barrage of clichés and repetitions, the bureaucratic and legalistic jargon, the omissions and circumlocutions of the witnesses. . . .

Political Doublespeak

Many Watergate witnesses were educated men, from the nation's finest schools, who used their skills in language to lie, to evade, to conceal, to confuse. So obvious was their manipulation that citizens who aren't normally interested in language matters recognized, vaguely at least, that language indeed was being used—either as a weapon or as a mask.

Within days after the Ervin committee hearings [chaired by Senator Sam Ervin (D-IL)] began on television, certain stock phrases *("at this point in time"),* words *("inoperative"),* metaphors *("game plan," "laundered money"),* and bureaucratic and legal jargon provided source material for political cartoonists, nightclub comedians, TV talk show hosts, and satirists of all sorts and degrees, from the professional to the barroom pundit. [Columnists and satirists] Herblock and "Doonesbury," Art Buchwald and Russell Baker, *Mad* and

National Lampoon had a heyday. It was a cornucopia of cant for satiric recycling.

Watergate was a war of words, a drama of language manipulation.

Even the more solemn Watergate watchers were astonished by the verbal performance. David Wise [author of *The Politics of Lying*] sent me his "favorite" Watergate quote—a 300-word answer by [Nixon assistant John] Ehrlichman (to a "yes-no" kind of question) in which the words simply flowed out, sidetracking, winding back and forth, looping around, eventually ending nowhere, a diversionary bit of rambling nonsense. In my judgment, one of the high spots (low spots?) of Watergate testimony was that of Patrick Buchanan, later described by *Time* as "quick-witted and fast talking . . . the Administration's most effective witness." A sampling, of Buchanan's effectiveness:

> Senator [Daniel] Inouye: "Do you think it's ethical?"
> (long pause)
> Buchanan: "I don't think it's unethical."
> Senator [Joseph] Montoya: "Do you think it's proper?"
> (long pause)
> Buchanan: "I don't think it's improper."

In George Orwell's famous essay, "Politics and the English Language," he thought that it "should be possible to laugh the not-un formation out of existence." Unfortunately, Orwell was wrong. Nobody laughed.

As [journalist and playwright] Richard Gambino wrote: "The torrent of circumlocutions, mechanical verbal formulas, misplaced technical jargon, palliative expressions, euphemisms, and inflated phraseology indicate that the brains both of speakers and listeners are being anesthetized or stunted. . . . It is often hard to tell whether they are merely dissemblers trying to paralyze the minds of others, self-deceivers who have crippled their own intelligences, or glib dolls whose characters remained undeveloped as their smartness grew."

Gambino suggested that the general emphasis on Watergate's sensational *1984* aspects (bugging, spying, etc.) obscured the importance of the ethical and moral irresponsibility which flourishes in the fertilizer of this debased language: "If our political language, and therefore our public thinking, becomes so debauched that moral meanings can no longer be clearly expressed, then all the gadgets, technology and techniques of Watergate will be unnecessary. We will have already slipped into a *1984* nightmare. A society that cannot speak or understand sense is condemned to live nonsensically."

Concealment and Omission Versus Overt Lies

But the dominant language problem of the whole Watergate affair was not what was said, but what was unsaid. Watergate essentially will be remembered as a classic example of concealment and secrecy, in all phases from the initial planning through all parts of the cover-up attempt. The language problem was that of omission, a more subtle kind of lying and deception than the "active" aggressive untruths we normally recognize as lies. . . .

Our society's Judeo-Christian heritage emphasizes the prohibition of active lying: "Thou shalt not bear false witness against thy neighbor." People well understand deliberate falsification, lying under oath, perjury. But very little attention is given by ministers, moralists, or churchgoers to passive deception, sins of omission, calculated silence and secrecy, evasions and half-truths. In fact, our society places high value on keeping quiet. Silence is golden. We make folk heroes out of those (including gangsters) who keep their mouths shut, who "stonewall it." And we label those who reveal the truth as *squealers, informers, tattletales,* and *stool pigeons.*

Citizens who aren't normally interested in language matters recognized . . . that language indeed was being used—either as a weapon or a mask.

We grow up with ambiguities: our parents tell us to "own up" to our own errors, sins, misdeeds, mistakes, violations. We are told to "fess up," "be honest," "tell the truth." Yet, at the same time, our parents tell us (and we tell our children) that we are not to tell on others, not to be a tattletale on our siblings, our classmates, our companions (and later) our fellow workers when they err, sin, or commit a crime.

Granted, there are problems and distinctions concerning such silence which need to be discussed by our moralists, but some people recognize that these attitudes, learned in childhood, to be "loyal" to our group, to keep our mouths shut, later serve the interests of those adult groups most eager to keep their operations as secret as possible: criminal organizations; inefficient or corrupt bureaucracies; corporations or governments that abuse power or exploit people.

The torrent of circumlocutions, mechanical verbal formulas, misplaced technical jargon, [and] euphemisms . . . indicate that the brains of both speakers and listeners are being anesthetized.

Much of the hatred of the press by Nixon and his supporters was not simply because the press was the messenger, the bearer of bad news, but because it helped expose the situation, it was the tattletale. The whole Watergate situation originated in the arrogance of a generation of expanded presidential power and was nurtured by an obsessive concern about secrecy, about plugging "leaks." After two years of exposés, the White House still spent much time trying to divert attention from the substance of the information and focus on the "leaks" and "squealers."

Thus we can see that the language issues in the first year of Watergate centered around "bad grammar" (deviations from standard usage), clichés, trite expressions, repetition of commonplace metaphors, parroting of bureaucratic jargon, a bit of outright perjury here and there, and a great deal of evasive circumlocution and unspoken truth. When the probers learned by accident of the White House tapes, a new phase began for Watergate word watchers. Here, suddenly, the illusions and fabrications, the images of the President and his associates, were devastated by their own words. The release of the transcripts in the spring of 1974 provoked three major controversies concerning language: Nixon's vulgarity; the editing and prior censorship of the documents; and the revelation of character conveyed by the words spoken in the Oval Office.

Language Turned Public
Opinion Against the President

Nixon's pedestrian vulgarity was no secret among his intimates, nor his enemies. . . . But a large audience of true believers, which Nixon so carefully cultivated, did not know these aspects of his personality, or would not believe the critics who pointed them out. To those who had believed in the "morality" of Nixon, who had long seen Nixon as the innocent victim of the slanderous attacks of the villainous press, the (expletives deleted) in the transcripts were shocking. Emmet John Hughes, one of President Eisenhower's aides, commented that ". . . the single word that first came to mind as I read these transcripts was 'vulgarity'—vulgarity of thought and vulgarity of conscience." Editors at the *Chicago Tribune* noted that the transcripts "provide a cultural shock. Presidents don't talk like city hall hacks, do they? But appearance—the ruffles and flourishes, the prim smile and Sunday services—confronted reality and lost."

Why such an intense reaction? For one thing, Nixon had set himself up for such a fall from grace through years of preaching and pieties. . . . Nixon's pious pronouncements would be remembered; in the 1960 TV debates with John F. Kennedy, Nixon attacked the language of Harry Truman, in words which would come back later to haunt Nixon:

> [Nixon] "It makes you realize that whoever is President is going to be a man that all the children of America will either look up to or will look down to. And I can only say that I'm very proud that President Eisenhower restored dignity and decency and, frankly, good language to the conduct of the presidency of the United States. And I only hope that should I win this election, that I could [see] to it that whenever any mother or father talks to his child, he can look at the man in the White House and say: 'Well, there is a man who maintains the kind of standards personally that I would want my child to follow.'"

More serious vulgarities were the intimations of ethnic slurs, especially anti-Semitism, in Nixon's informal White House conversation among colleagues. After the initial release of the transcripts, rumors that some of the deletions contained derogatory remarks (such as "Jew boy," "kike," and "wop") were denied by the White House as another example of irresponsible press coverage. But the allegations were substantiated in August when other transcripts were yielded by Nixon in compliance with the Supreme Court order. Although the critical legal evidence from these transcripts was Nixon's early knowledge of the Watergate break-in and approval of a cover-up, magazines and newspapers noted these documents included a Nixon remark that his daughter ought to avoid public appearances at anything concerned with "the arts . . . the arts you know— they're Jews, they're left wing."

Ethical and moral irresponsibility . . . flourishes in the fertilizer of this debased language. . . . A society that cannot speak or understand sense is condemned to live nonsensically.

Nixon's "jocko-macho" talk (as [*New York Observer* columnist] Nicholas von Hoffman called it) was amply demonstrated; the limited supply of tough-guy metaphors, akin to verbal locker room swaggering of muscle-flexing machismo at the beach: *"tough it out," "stonewall it," "trade off," "head to head . . . zone defense," "let it hang out," "bottom-line it."* Years earlier, some critics had felt that Nixon's overt enthusiasm for spectator sports (shaking hands with athletes, telegrams and phone calls to coaches) was simply a calculated ploy ("a grandstand play") to win the favor of certain voters, to create the illusion that he was "just one of the guys." It was no illusion. Nixon was not the first politician to use the imagery of athletics . . . but the transcripts reveal that the traditional emphasis on "fair play," "following the rules," and "good sportsmanship" had been replaced by a "win at all costs" mentality.

From the moment that the White House version of the transcripts was originally released, the massive number (almost 1,900) of omissions, "expletives deleted . . . characterization deleted," and deletions "for national security reasons" or "unrelated material" made the transcripts suspect. If Nixon would release such damning material, how much more damning was that still concealed? Such inferences were widespread at the time. Were they reasonable?

Aristotle, some 2500 years ago, as the first major rhetorician teaching the art of persuasion, pointed out some of the common axioms used in persuasion: "If the less probable of two events has occurred," he said, "the more probable event is likely to have occurred too." Because rhetoric is involved in cases where there is doubt and disagreement (instead of certitude), Aristotle continued with a series of common arguments which people use in order to make reasonable judgments: "If someone had the power and the desire and the opportunity to do something," Aristotle continued, "then he has done it." In other words, people have long recognized the validity of overwhelming circumstantial evidence in cases which will not yield to certitude because the statements or opinions of the various parties involved are in conflict.

The [dominant] language problem was that of omission, a more subtle kind of lying and deception than the "active" aggressive untruths we normally recognize as lies.

The initial mistrust of the edited transcripts was confirmed by subsequent events: two months later, in July, the House Judiciary Committee issued its version of the transcripts, based on a more sophisticated technical analysis of the tapes. Although Chairman Peter Rodino did not accuse the White House staff of deliberate distortion, the evidence indicated that the "errors" and "accidental omissions" benefited Nixon. (Further evidence of the unreliability of the White House transcripts was provided a month later, August 5, when the President was forced by the Supreme Court to surrender other tapes which, by his admission, were "at variance" with his earlier public statements; three days later Nixon resigned.) . . .

Speech Reveals Characters

The primary impact of the transcripts (both the White House version and the more revealing version from the Rodino committee) was that they laid bare the President's character. The May 1974 issues of the nation's newspapers and magazines were saturated with violent and bitter commentary about the transcripts, indicating that a shocked, angered, and sorrowed nation did not hesitate to infer the caliber of Nixon's character from the words which had been revealed. Almost unanimously, the assessment of Richard Nixon's character was rather harsh, even from those who once had been loyal supporters, but who now felt that they had been betrayed. Republican Senator Hugh Scott, who had earlier predicted that the transcripts would vindicate Nixon, was one of the first to express his disillusionment: "shabby, disgusting, immoral." Throughout the country these sentiments were echoed in an intense outpouring of criticism and analysis of Nixon's character as revealed in the transcripts. In the future, one must remember that in May 1974, Nixon was still a powerful protagonist; after his resignation and loss of power, he was seen by many as a pathetic figure, one inspiring pathos, and the tone and temper of subsequent criticism against him differed after "this point in time."

For years to come . . . Watergate transcripts will be alluded to in the classrooms [to] explain and illustrate [the] practice of inferring character from speech.

In the previous year, at the November 1973 convention of the National Council of Teachers of English, Walker Gibson, delivering his presidential address to that group, pointed out some links between the teaching of literature in the classroom and the analysis of the ongoing Watergate investigation. "When we read *Hamlet*, or *Charlotte's Web*, or whatever it may be," Gibson said, "we infer dramatic character from language. Because Hamlet says the things he says, in the way he is made to say them, we conclude that he is this or that sort of a person, and we have our evidence before us in the words on the page or stage. Learning to read is learning to infer dramatic character from linguistic evidence." Gibson then made some analysis of the Watergate hearings, of both the witnesses and the senators, and of some of the inferences one could make from their language: "What does it say, for example, about a person's attitude toward law and order if, when describing some a clearly illegal act by a White House colleague, he calls the act inappropriate?"

At that time, Gibson was speaking about the publicly

known Watergate testimony as witnessed on TV. No one knew then that the very words of the President in the Oval Office were being tape-recorded, and that they would eventually become public. Gibson's point is even more germane when one considers the impact of the transcripts. [Historian and urban planner] Louis Mumford, for example, said that he felt as if Nixon had "committed moral suicide in public" when the transcripts were released. Carey McWilliams, writing in the *Nation* (May 18 [1974]), ironically commented: "The Nixon of the transcripts is an authentic person. It is refreshing to listen to the real private voice after years of exposure to the public television voice and manner. The transcripts contain his words and phrases. This is the way he thinks. No PR fakery, no television smirking, no smug self-righteous rhetoric. . . . This is a hard-bitten operator, a political huckster, a man on the make and obsessed with making it." The differences between a person's public and private voices (or personae) has long been an intriguing topic for teachers of language and literature. For years to come, it seems certain that the Watergate transcripts will be alluded to in the classrooms as teachers explain and illustrate this practice of inferring character from speech.

Language Can Be Manipulated

Another lesson which should be learned from Watergate, and which can be taught in the classroom, is that language can be manipulated to downplay, to hide, to conceal, to omit. More attention can be given, in a kind of "defensive rhetoric," to teaching students how to recognize the strategies of silence, the tactics of omission, evasion, diversion, circumlocution.

Another lesson which should be learned from Watergate . . . is that language can be manipulated to downplay, to hide, to conceal, to omit.

Hopefully, one of the political lessons which can be learned by all citizens is the need for comprehensive disclosure laws, codes of ethics, open information laws by which political groups, commercial corporations, and governments at all levels must reveal full, clear, understandable information about their financing and operations. Citizens and consumers will eventually recognize that all of the various "Truth-in-" laws (lending, packaging, advertising, etc.) are related to this basic concept of full disclosure. At present, the privacy of the individual citizen is being invaded at the same time the secrecy of the corporate structure is being protected; this trend must be reversed. Perhaps, one way to start is in the classroom, by making students aware of these patterns of concealment. . . .

Hopefully, young people will grow up in this generation with fewer illusions, with fewer romanticized myths about our history and our politics, with a greater awareness of how fragile democracy can be. Hopefully, the schools will recognize that our future citizens need a more sophisticated literacy, a literacy which includes training in the critical analysis of propaganda techniques, language manipulation, and the new media.

Chronology

1972

June 17: Burglars attempt to break into the offices of the Democratic National Committee (DNC) headquarters located in the Watergate office complex in Washington, D.C. One of the five burglars arrested is former CIA agent James McCord.

June 19: Two men co-indicted with the suspected Watergate burglars, G. Gordon Liddy and E. Howard Hunt, are identified as White House aides to Republican incumbent Richard Nixon. Former attorney general John Mitchell, coordinator of the Committee to Reelect the President (CRP), denies any link to the operation.

August 1: A cashier's check in the amount of $25,000 that should have been deposited in the Nixon reelection fund is deposited into the bank account of a Watergate burglar.

October 10: The FBI implicates CRP in the Watergate break-in, charging that CRP conducted a widespread campaign of political dirty tricks on behalf of Nixon's reelection campaign.

November 7: Nixon is reelected in one of the largest presidential election landslides in history, taking more than 60 percent of the popular vote.

1973

January 8–30: The trial of the Watergate burglars. A jury finds McCord and Liddy guilty; the five actual burglars enter guilty pleas.

February 7: The Senate Select Committee on Presidential Campaign Activities, later renamed the Senate Watergate Committee, is formed to investigate illegal, improper, and unethical activities possibly committed during the 1972 presidential campaign.

March 25–29: Under oath before the Senate Watergate

Committee, McCord delivers a new version of the Watergate burglary. McCord testifies former Nixon aide Jeb Magruder and White House counsel John Dean both knew of the plans to illegally enter DNC and bug the headquarters. He also states that Liddy told him that Mitchell had approved the plans, and that Charles Colson, a former special counsel to the president, was also aware of the plans. The burglary is increasingly viewed as a conspiracy at high levels, and the investigation expands.

May 18: The Senate Watergate Committee conducts nationally televised hearings as part of the Watergate investigation. Attorney General Elliot Richardson appoints former solicitor general Archibald Cox as the Justice Department's special prosecutor.

June 25: Dean implicates Nixon in efforts to cover up his administration's knowledge of the Watergate burglary.

July 10: Mitchell contradicts testimony by McCord and Dean, insisting that he did not approve the Watergate burglary and that Nixon had no knowledge of the subsequent cover-up attempt by members of his administration.

July 13: Testimony before the Senate Watergate Committee reveals that Nixon taped all of his conversations and telephone calls on a secret oval office taping system. Nixon orders the system disconnected a few days later. The committee and Cox subpoena the tapes.

July 23: Nixon refuses to produce the subpoenaed tapes.

October 10: Vice President Spiro Agnew resigns under allegations of income tax evasion. Although he was not implicated in the mounting Watergate scandal, his resignation adds to the negative public image of the Nixon administration.

October 13: The House Judiciary Committee begins hearings to confirm House Minority Leader Gerald Ford as vice president.

October 20: Cox refuses a presidential order to cease his attempts to subpoena the secret White House tapes. Nixon orders Richardson to fire Cox. Richardson refuses and resigns. Nixon orders Deputy Attorney General William Ruckleshaus to fire Cox. Ruckleshaus also refuses and is fired by Nixon. Solicitor General Robert H. Bork becomes acting attorney general, complies with Nixon's order, and fires Cox. The events become known as the "Saturday Night Massacre."

October 23: The House Judiciary Committee initiates procedures for an impeachment proceeding against Nixon.

November 1: Bork appoints Texas attorney Leon Jaworski as the new special prosecutor.

November 17: Nixon, in a nationally televised press conference, announces, "I am not a crook." He turns over the subpoenaed tapes as evidence of his willingness to cooperate with the Senate Watergate Committee.

November 27: Ford is confirmed as the new vice president.

December 7: The House Judiciary Committee reviewing nine subpoenaed taped conversations between Nixon and his aides, discover an 18½-minute gap in one of the tapes; White House explanation of the deletion as unintentional secretarial error is met with widespread skepticism.

1974

March 1: Nixon administration officials and aides John Mitchell, H.R. Haldeman, John Ehrlichman, Charles Colson, Robert C. Mardian, Kenneth W. Parkinson, and Gordon Strachan are indicted by a federal grand jury for their participation in hindering the Watergate burglary investigation. Nixon is also named as an unindicted co-conspirator.

April 11: The House Judiciary Committee subpoenas the remaining forty-two secret White House tapes.

April 29: In a nationally televised broadcast, Nixon responds to the subpoena by stating he will release only edited transcripts of the requested tapes in the interests of national security. Nixon's refusal to supply the tapes prompts special prosecutor Jaworski to argue the subpoena in front of the Supreme Court.

May 9: The House Judiciary Committee opens formal impeachment proceedings against the president.

July 24: The Supreme Court rules that Nixon does not have the authority to submit edited transcripts in lieu of the subpoenaed tapes, and orders him to surrender the tapes to the special prosecutor. Nixon complies with the request.

July 24–30: The House Judiciary Committee adopts three

articles of impeachment: obstruction of justice, abuse of power, and noncompliance with subpoenas.

August 5: Transcripts of the subpoenaed tapes reveal that Nixon had attempted to hinder the investigation into the Watergate break-in.

August 9: Nixon becomes the first president in U.S. history to resign from office. Vice President Gerald Ford is sworn in as president.

September 8: Ford pardons Nixon for all crimes that he committed or that he may have committed while in office.

For Further Research

Books

Carl Bernstein and Bob Woodward, *All the President's Men.* New York: Warner, 1976.

James M. Cannon, *Time and Chance: Gerald Ford's Appointment with History.* New York: HarperCollins, 1994.

Len Colodny and Robert Gettlin, *Silent Coup: The Removal of a President.* New York: St. Martin's, 1991.

John Ehrlichman, *Witness to Power: The Nixon Years.* New York: Simon & Schuster, 1982.

Barbara Silberdick Feinberg, *Watergate: Scandal in the White House.* New York: Watts, 1990.

Herbert Foerstel, *From Watergate to Monicagate: Ten Controversies in Modern Journalism and Media.* Westport, CT: Greenwood, 2001.

Leonard Garment, *In Search of Deep Throat.* New York: Basic Books, 2000.

Michael A. Genovese, *The Watergate Crisis.* Westport, CT: Greenwood, 1999.

Leon Jaworski, *The Right and the Power: The Prosecution of Watergate.* New York: Reader's Digest Press, 1976.

Stanley I. Kutler, *The Wars of Watergate: The Last Crisis of Richard Nixon.* New York: Knopf, 1990.

G. Gordon Liddy, *Will: The Autobiography of G. Gordon Liddy.* New York: St. Martin's, 1990.

Anthony Summers, *The Arrogance of Power: The Secret World of Richard Nixon.* New York: Viking, 2000.

Bob Woodward, *Shadow: Five Presidents and the Legacy of Watergate.* New York: Simon & Schuster, 1999.

Jerry Zeifman, *Without Honor: The Crimes of Camelot and the Impeachment of President Nixon.* New York: Thunder's Mouth, 1996.

Web Sites

History Place: Presidential Impeachment Hearings, www. historyplace.com/unitedstates/impeachments/nixon.htm. This Web site offers a detailed account of the impeachment proceedings against President Richard Nixon. Included is a copy of the articles of impeachment.

Houston Chronicle's 25th Anniversary of Watergate, www. chron.com/content/interactive/special/watergate. Links to articles, speeches, and other documents related to Watergate and its impact on American culture. Documents available for viewing include Nixon's presidential papers, an audio file of Nixon's "I am not a crook" speech, and a quiz to test one's knowledge of Watergate events.

Illusion and Delusion: The Watergate Decade, www.musarium.com/watergate.html. Sponsored by Musarium, a site dedicated to photographing important historical and cultural events, *Illusion and Delusion* is a photo essay of the 1970s. Events highlighted include Nixon's historic trip to China, the passage of the Equal Rights Amendment, and several of the events surrounding Watergate.

Time News File: Watergate, www.time.com/time/newsfiles/watergate. *Time* magazine's Web page on Watergate is devoted to issues of *Time* that featured important stories on the events of Watergate as they unfolded in the media. Also featured are magazine articles that examine the events of Nixon's life both before and after the Watergate scandal.

WashingtonPost.com: Revisiting Watergate, www.washingtonpost.com/wp-srv/national/longterm/watergate. The *Washington Post* was one of the first newspapers to cover the Watergate story at length, and, famously, the first to report significant connections between the Watergate burglars and the Nixon administration. This Web site marks the twenty-fifth anniversary of Watergate and features a selection of articles including primary sources from the Watergate era as well as current reflections by reporters and editors who participated in the journalistic investigation.

Index